Simplified Accounts

A Basic Guide

By Gwen Harlow

Acknowledgements

The author would like to thank the former examining boards named below, who gave permission to use exam questions from past papers. The examining boards are the copyright holders.

The Northern Ireland Schools Examination and Assessment Council very kindly provided the author with their marking schemes. The other boards are in no way responsible for the answers given. The London East Anglian Group accepts no responsibility whatsoever for the accuracy or method of working in the answers given.

In all cases, the answers given may not necessarily constitute the only possible solutions.

The London East Anglian Group

The Northern Examining Association

Northern Ireland Schools Examinations and Assessment Council

© by Gwen Harlow 2007. All rights reserved.

ISBN 978-1-84753-638-9

Preface

This book is a practical step by step approach to book-keeping and accounts. It was originally written to help students with examinations, so some minor revisions have been made to some of the chapters, to make it a more general guide. Some old exam questions have still been used for training attempts, as they are relatively simple and will help the reader to check his or her progress.

Accounting is essentially a very practical subject, and requires much practice. Therefore each chapter throughout contains questions for the reader to test themselves. All the answers are in the back of the book. Exam questions are still used, in spite of the demise of the exam, because these are good simple tests.

In real life, things tend to be much more complex with lots of anomalies and so on. Different firms have their own ways of setting out accounts, and in any case most use computer programs. However, having learnt the basics, it should be possible to understand what the computer has done!

You may have wondered what the difference is between book-keeping and accounting, and why both terms are used. Book-keeping refers to the day-to-day recording of sales, purchases, returned goods and payments. Accounting is the bringing together of all these figures in totals. For example the book-keeper will have worked out the total sales figure for a given time (probably one year), and the accountant will then use this figure to work out the profit. Various other total figures are also provided by the book-keeper.

In order to provide this information accurately and efficiently, it is obvious that there must be an organised system of book-keeping. The most widely used system throughout the western world is called double entry book-keeping. It is not a new idea. In fact it was described in a text book written by an Italian called Luca Pacioli in 1494.

Debit and credit in book-keeping do not necessarily mean the same things as in ordinary English. The debits and credits are the opposite way around from those found in your bank account, because these accounts are from your point of view, whereas the bank statement is from the bank's point of view. Some people find this a little difficult at first.
If you work your way through the book doing all the exercises, you should have a good basic grounding by the end.

G M Harlow

Contents

	Acknowledgements	2
	Preface	3
	List of illustrations	5
1	The cash book	7
2	Double entry book-keeping	18
3	Trial balance	39
4	Trading and profit and loss accounts	45
5	The balance sheet	55
6	Accounting for depreciation	60
7	Bad debts	69
8	Manufacturing accounts	74
9	Club accounts	80
10	Partnerships	84
11	Appropriation accounts of Plc and Ltd	94
12	Interpretation of final accounts	101
13	Funds Flow statements	108
14	Incomplete Records	113
15	Mark up and margin	119
16	Bank Reconciliation	123
17	Petty cash	129
18	Break even analysis	135
19	Cash budgets	139
	Answers to the exercises	142
	Accounting concepts	190
	Glossary	191
	Index	194

List of Illustrations

1	Cash Book: debit and credit	8
2	Cash and bank columns	8
3	Debit and credit entries	9
4	Writing up a cash book	9
5	How to balance a cash book	11
6	Entering discounts	14
7	Cash and bank accounts	20
8	Making a contra entry	22
9	Double entry procedure	25
10	Sales and purchases on credit	27
11	Sales day book	33
12	Purchases day book	35
13	Recording in the journal	41
14	Balance sheet showing depreciation	64
15	Entering depreciation on the asset account	66
16	Provision for depreciation	66
17	A disposal account	68
18	Debiting provision for bad debts	70
19	Crediting provision for bad debts	71
20	Bad debts provision in the balance sheet	71
21	From manufacturing to profit and loss	78
22	Receipts and payments	81
23	Income and expenditure	81
24	Appropriation account	87
25	Partnership capital and current accounts	89
26	Shares on the balance sheet	99
27	Preparation for flow of funds statement	109
28	Flow of funds statement	110
29	Practice sheet for flow of funds (1)	111
30	Practice sheet for flow of funds (2)	112
31	Cash book	116
32	Mark up and margin	120
33	Reconciling cash book to bank statement	124
34	Exercise in reconciliation	127
35	Reconciliation exercise	128

List of illustrations

36	Petty cash voucher	130
37	Petty cash book	131
38	Petty cash book example	131
39	Petty cash book exercise	133
40	Break even chart	136
41	Break even exercise	138
42	Cash budget chart	140
43	Cash budget exercise	141
44	Answer for chapter 1	143
45	Answer for chapter 1	143
46	Answer for chapter 1	144
47	Answer for chapter 1	145
48	Answer for chapter 2	147
49	Answer for chapter 2	148
50	Answer for chapter 2	150
51	Answer for chapter 2	151
52	Answer for chapter 2	152
53	Answer for chapter 2	154
54	Answer for chapter 6	163
55	Answer for chapter 7	165
56	Answer for chapter 7	165
57	Answer for chapter 7	166
58	Answer for chapter 10	173
59	Answer for chapter 16	182
60	Answer for chapter 17	184
61	Answer for chapter 17	185
62	Answer for chapter 18	186
63	Answer for chapter 18	187
64	Answer for chapter 19	189

1
The Cash Book

The basis of accounting is money. Monetary transactions are recorded in the cash book. In some very small businesses, the cash book is virtually all the book–keeping that is done. The cash book is known as a book of original entry. This means that it is the first place where items are recorded. The cash book contains two accounts: the cash account and the bank account. Do not confuse this with the bank account held at the bank. This bank account is the business's own record. There are firms who use the cash book solely as a reference, and they keep separate cash and bank accounts elsewhere. In this book the cash book will be treated as being the only place where the two accounts are recorded. This is the most common method.

You will learn about other books of original entry and all the accounts as you progress. Do not worry if all these names seem strange to you just now. Students are often terrified at the thought of learning so many new things, but you will learn all that you need to know gradually.

WHAT DOES THE CASH BOOK DO ?

The cash book records the money coming in and going out: the 'ins' on the left and the 'outs' on the right.' In' is known as debit,' out' is known as credit. This is opposite to what you have been used to in your personal bank account! This is because the bank prints its statements from its own point of view, i.e. a debit is in their favour ('in' as far as the bank is concerned), and a credit is in your favour ('out' as far as the bank is concerned). Many people find this confusing when first writing up their own business accounts.

If you have sold goods for cash of £50, you will enter the £50 in the debit (in) side of the cash book. If you then pay your suppliers £30, this will be entered in the credit (out) side of the cash book.

Debit (In)		Credit (Out)	
Cash Sales	50.00	Paid suppliers	30.00

Fig. 1. The Simplest Cash Book: debit and credit

Some of the money will be in cash, some in cheques and other bank transactions. You will therefore have separate columns for cash and bank in the cash book. It will look like the example in Figure 2.

Debit (In)			Credit (Out)		
Details	Cash	Bank	Details	Cash	Bank

Fig. 2. Cash and Bank columns

If you receive a cheque from someone it will go in the bank column on the left. If you pay a cheque out this goes in the bank column on the right. Suppose you receive £50 in cash sales, pay £30 to suppliers in cash, receive a cheque for £45 and pay a cheque to someone for £40.

The cash book would look like the one in Fig 3.

Details	Cash	Bank	Details	Cash	Bank
Cash Sales Received cheque	50.00	45.00	Paid Suppliers Paid cheque	30.00	40.00

Fig.3. Showing the cash and bank columns with entries for both

Suppose Henry Smith runs a gardening service.

April 1   Henry received a cheque for £50 from Mrs Dawson for gardening work.

April 2   On the 2nd April he paid £30 cheque to have his mower repaired.

April 6   He received £10 cash from Emma Jones for work done.

Aril 10   He paid £8 in cash for petrol.

Mar 31   He had £10 cash and £35 in the bank.

His cash book for April can be seen in Fig 4.

Date	Details	Cash	Bank	Date	Details	Cash	Bank
Apr 1 Apr 6	Bal. b/d M.Dawson E. Jones	10.00 10.00	35.00 50.00	Apr 2 Apr 10	Mowr.repar Petrol	8.00	30.00

Fig. 4. Writing up the cash book

Now try an exercise yourself

Enter these transactions in the cash book for June. The opening balances (the amounts already in the accounts) were £30 debit bank and £25 debit cash.

June 1   Cash sales £30
June 2   Paid rent £40 cheque
June 5   Bought goods for cash £10
June 9   Paid telephone bill of £50 by cheque
June 11 Received cheque for £75
June 17 Paid window cleaner cash £5

When you have entered these items you have to 'balance' them up. This means you add them up to see how much you have left. The way to do it is this:

- You rule a line across the bottom of the page, but leaving a line above it free.
- You add each column in the book, putting the totals in pencil at the bottom. The larger totals are the ones to be inked in.
- The totals must always be the same on the other side. If you have £10 cash on the left, but £7 cash on the right you must ink in £10 total for both left and right cash columns.
- Therefore you will have some columns which add up to less than the total you have inked in.

This is what is meant by balancing.

You left a line free above the totals. Put in here the amount needed to make the column equal the total at the bottom. Look at the example.

Note that c/d means carried down and b/d means brought down.

The figure you put in (balancing figure) is always brought down to the opposite side. To do this you must write the amount under the totals box on the opposite side with the abbreviation b/d in front of it.

The figures that are brought down represent what the business has in that account. In the example, the figures brought down are £12 cash and £50 bank, both on the left. Remember that left is the 'in' side of the book. This means that there is £12 in cash and £50 in the bank. Sometimes this figure differs with that on the bank statement from the bank. Your records will not always agree with those at the bank. There are various reasons for this, dealt with in Chapter 16 on bank reconciliation.

It sometimes happens that balances are brought down to the right–hand side, the 'out' side. If this is the bank column it means that you have overdrawn, taken more than you have in the account. This should not, of course, happen with the cash unless your cash box contains i.o.u. notes!

Fig. 5. How to balance a cash book

Stage 1

Date	Details	Cash	Bank	Date	Details	Cash	Bank
Apr 1	Bal. b/d	10.00	35.00				
			50.00	Apr 2	Mowr.repar		30.00
Apr 6	M.Dawson	10.00		Apr 10	Petrol	8.00	
	E. Jones				To c/d	?	?
		20.00	85.00			20.00	85.00

Stage 2

Date	Details	Cash	Bank	Date	Details	Cash	Bank
Apr 1	Bal. b/d	10.00	35.00				
			50.00	Apr 2	Mow.repair		30.00
Apr 6	M.Dawson	10.00		Apr 10	Petrol	8.00	
	E. Jones						
					To c/d	12.00	55.00
		20.00	85.00			20.00	85.00
	b/d	12.00	55.00				

An exercise to check your progress:

June 1   Gemma Jackson has £30 in the bank and £5 in her cash box.

June 3   She received a cheque for £10.

June 5   She took £25 in cash sales.

June 6   She paid £35 cheque for her rent and had £10 in cash sales.

June 10   She paid a part time assistant £20 cash.

June 12   She took £20 in cash sales, and paid her supplier a cheque for £40.

Write up the cash book and bring the balances down.

SUMMARY

- Debit = Income
- Credit = Expenses(Outgoings)
- Totals of both sides must be the same
- Balancing figure is brought down on opposite side

Discounts

There is another main column which is included in most cash books.

Trade discount

This is a large discount given to other traders. It is given for two main reasons: bulk purchases, and to allow the other trader to make a profit. It is deducted from the customer's bill (invoice) before entering the invoice in the accounts.

Cash discount

Sometimes customers are offered cash discount for prompt payment. On the bottom of their bill (invoice) you may see the words 5% discount if paid within 30 days. These terms vary of course, but that would be a typical one. It is not deducted until the customer pays. He will deduct it from his payment if he has paid within the time allowed. This is the discount that is entered in the cash book. It is entered in the discounts allowed column.

You also receive cash discount when you pay your suppliers (if you pay promptly). This goes in the discounts received column.

        i   discounts allowed on the left
        i   discounts received on the right.

Think of their initials 'a' and 'r' and just remember that 'a' is first in the alphabet. You now have a three column cash book.

So if Gemma receives a cheque from a customer for £19 in full settlement of their account of £20, they have taken discount of £1. If she pays a supplier £14.25 in full settlement of her account of £15, she has taken discount of £0.75. It will be shown as in Fig 6.

Note that discount columns are not balanced. The totals are entered in discount accounts. You will learn more of that later.

Date	Details	Discount	Cash	Bank	Date	Details	Discount	Cash	Bank
	chq	1.00		19.00		Chq paid out	0.75		14.25

Fig. 6. Entering discounts

Exercise using a three column cash book.

June 30   Gemma's balances were debit cash £40 and credit bank £35.

July 1   She received a cheque for £38 in full settlement of a customer's account of £40.

July 4   She received £30 in cash sales which she immediately paid into the bank.

July 15   She paid a supplier 23.75 in full settlement of her account of £25.

July 20   There were further cash sales of £10.

July 25   She paid her cleaner £20 cash.

Write up the cash book and bring the balances down.

There are further columns which may be added to the cash book to suit any individual firm's requirements. However, the three shown are the main ones. Once you are familiar with these, it will be a simple matter to add to them. Do not move on to the next chapter unless you have been successful in the exercises, and understand the summary and the checklist below.

Contra Entries

It is sometimes necessary to make transfers from cash into bank and vice versa. The entries you make in the cash book are accompanied by a small c. For example if you wish to transfer £50 from cash into bank then the entries you make are debit bank and credit cash. Each £50 will be written as c50 in the cash book. It simply means that the entries are equal and cancel each other out. They are known as contra entries. See Fig.8.

CHECKLIST AND TEST

- What is the purpose of the cash book?
- Are you able to enter and balance cash book?
- What do the balances tell you?
- What is the difference between cash discount and trade discount?
- How does this affect the cash book?

Check your progress

The following question is from the Northern Ireland schools Summer 1989 GCSE Exam. Note that the final part of the question has been omitted from here, but appears in the bank reconciliation chapter later in the book.

During the first week of March 1989 Mourne Enterprises had the following cash and bank transactions:

On 1 March Cash in Hand was £50, while the bank account was £1150 overdrawn.

On 2 March Sales of £2,400 were paid straight into the bank.

On 3 March £28 was paid in cash to Cleaners; also an amount of £1,000 owed to a supplier, P.Murphy, was paid by cheque.

On 4 March a debtor, W.Scott, paid by cheque £540, taking advantage of a £5 discount; on the same date £40 cash was taken out of the bank for office use.

On 5 March Salaries were paid by cheque £440.

Required

- Enter the above transactions in the firm's Cash Book for the first week of March 1989.
- Bring down the new balances.
- Explain the meaning of the new balances.
- Why is cash discount given to debtors?
- Explain the meaning of a 'contra entry.'

(Answers to questions throughout the book are given in Chapter 21)

Analysis Cash Book

There is an alternative style of cash book, with multiple columns on the right hand side. This style is ideal for 'cash accounting' where all transactions are paid immediately or very quickly. When filling in tax forms for the business, you have the option to select cash accounting rather than accruals. Accruals accounting is where people will owe you money from month to month and therefore there are always items hanging over from the previous month.

The columns on the right of this book will refer to your expense items, such as vehicle maintenance, repairs and renewals, plant hire, stationery and so on. These will vary according to the nature of the business. At any given time, you will be able to check how much these items are costing, by the totals at the foot of the last page.

If you use this type of cash book, there will be also be a grand total of all the columns on each side, and these totals will be brought forward in the same way as illustrated for the other types of cash book.

2

Double Entry Book–Keeping

Double entry simply means that for every entry you make, there has to be a corresponding opposite entry. This means that if you make a debit entry in the cash book, you must make a credit entry somewhere else.

Let's suppose that a friend of ours, John Moss, is going into business selling vegetables on a market stall. He decides to start the business off with £1000, and uses this to open a bank account for the business. The first entry will be debit cash book £1000. Following the double entry system you will then have to credit an account. The account you will credit is the capital account.

The capital account represents what the business owes to the owner. This may sound strange, but is in accordance with an important accounting concept.

ACCOUNTING CONCEPTS

All accounting is done in accordance with certain principles or concepts. These will be explained as they arise in the course of the work. Also there is a list in chapter 22 for quick reference.

You have now encountered two concepts.

1. Duality. Double entry: debit and credit for every transaction.
2. Business Entity. The business is a separate entity from the owner. This can be hard for many people to understand.

The Business Entity concept helps to explain why the business should owe John anything. Many people would regard the business as being John anyway, but this is not so. This is why John must always keep his own private bank account completely separate from that of the business.

So the first entries have been made. Now suppose that John decides to buy a second-hand van for £500, and pays by cheque.

The double entry for this will be:

- credit cash book bank column
- debit an account you will start and call motor van account.

The purchases account

Next John goes to a nearby large wholesale market to buy some produce. He spends £250, paying by cheque. The double entry for this is

- credit bank (in cash book)
- debit an account you will call purchases.

The purchases account will be used to record all purchases made for resale.

Note that the purchase of the van did not go into purchases account. This is because the van is going to be kept by the business. It is known as an asset. Assets are such things as premises, motor vehicles, machinery, fixtures and fittings and furniture. You will learn more about these later. For the moment, just be aware that only purchases for resale (or materials to be made into goods for resale) are to be entered onto the purchases account.

Setting up different accounts

Now suppose that John goes to market and sells his produce for £320.

The entry for that will be:

- debit the cash book cash column
- credit to an account he will call sales .

John now has to pay rent for his stall of £20. He pays cash. The entry for this will be:

- credit cash column in the cash book
- debit rent account.

He has now started a cash book and five different accounts.

Fig. 7. Accounts written in three column running balance style.
Cash Book

Date	Details	Cash	Bank	Date	Details	Cash	Bank
	Capital		1000		Van		500
	Sales	320			Produce		250
					Rent	20	
					To c/d	300	250
		320	1000			320	1000
	b/d	300	250				

Capital Account

Date	Details	Debit	Credit	Balance
	Bank		1000	1000cr.

Motor Van Account

Date	Details	Debit	Credit	Balance
	Bank	500		500

Purchases Account

Date	Details	Debit	Credit	Balance
	Bought produce	250		250

Sales Account

Date	Details	Debit	Credit	Balance
	Cash Sales		320	320

Rent Account

Date	Details	Debit	Credit	Balance
	Bank	20		20

Fig. 7b. The accounts could all be written up like the example below:

Alternative style:

Rent Account

    Dr   Cr

    20

           to   c/d   20

    20   20

b/d 20

> Note that the accounts can take one of two forms. In real life they are usually the three column, running balance type, within a computer program. This has been so for many years now. Many people find the accounts easier to understand that way, which is why it is used for bank statements.
>
> If you have to write up a lot of accounts by hand, or just for an exercise, it may be simpler to write them with the debits and credits side by side as in the cash book. You may do them whichever way you wish.

Contra Entry

You will see that the business now has £300 in cash and £250 in the bank. John may decide to pay most of the cash into the bank, say £250. The double entry for this will be

- debit the column bank
- credit cash – out of cash into bank.

When making an entry like this in the cash book you mark the entries with a small c as shown in Fig 8 and described in Chapter 1. The c stands for contra. This is known as a contra entry.

Making a contra entry:
Cash Book

Date	Details	Cash	Bank	Date	Details	Cash	Bank
	Balance b/d	300	250				
	Cash		c250		Bank	c 250	
					To c/d	50	500
		300	500			300	500
	b/d	50	500				

Fig. 8.

As you will see, the business now has £50 in cash and £500 in the bank.

Now see if you can make a few entries for John.

Suppose he does the following :–

- Buys more produce for £350 by cheque
- Sells more for £515 cash
- Pays rent again of £20 cash
- Buys new scales and pays £150 cheque
- Pays petrol bill £50 cash

How should these be entered ? If you didn't get that right, go back to the beginning of the chapter and follow it through again.

CHECKLIST

1. Do you know what the Duality Accounting concept means?
2. Do you know what Business Entity means?
3. Only certain purchases are entered on the purchases account. Do you know what these are?
4. What is the double entry for cash sales?

SALES AND PURCHASES ON CREDIT

So far all the entries made have been easy to work out, as they all went through the cash book. As you know which is in and out in the cash book, it was easy to know which side the other half of the double entry should be.

Unfortunately, life is not always so simple. People do not always pay straight away. This is the main reason for keeping so many accounts.

If you go into a shop to buy a jar of coffee, you pay the shop, take the coffee and that is that. The shop does not need to have an account for you. The double entry would be:

- debit their cash book

- credit their sales account (with the total sales for the day).

However, if you do not pay straight away for a suite of furniture or a television, the shop will need to keep a record of you. This will be an account in their sales ledger. The double entry would not affect the cash book. *You can only put items through the cash book where immediate payment is involved.* The double entry for the furniture would be

- debit the customer's account (in place of cash book)

- credit sales account as usual.

In your own accounts, your purchase of furniture would go into your purchase ledger. You would open an account in your purchase ledger for the shop you bought it from. The double entry in your accounts would be

- credit the supplier (in place of the cash book)

- debit your furniture account. (Not purchases unless you were selling furniture in the course of your business.)

Study Fig 9 to see which ledger the accounts belong to. Customers in sales (debtors) ledger, suppliers in purchase (bought or creditors) ledger, and everything else in the nominal (or general) ledger. Some firms do split the nominal into assets (real) ledger and expenses. Also some firms keep a private ledger for the owner's capital and other accounts he doesn't want the junior accounts staff to know about. For this book you need only concern yourself with sales, purchases and the one nominal (general) ledger. The names in brackets are alternative names which you need to be aware of.

Fig 9 Double entry Procedure

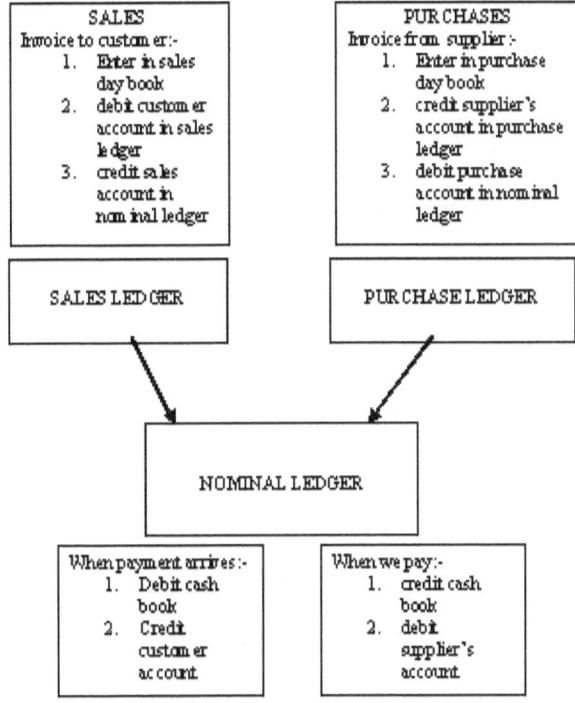

An exercise in sales and purchases on credit:

Sally Marshall starts a business as follows:

- Began by putting £3600 in the bank
- Bought some office furniture by cheque £650
- Bought machinery £550 on credit from Armitage Ltd. (For use in the business)
- Takings from cash sales £58

- Sold goods on credit to B.Wilson for £72.
- Paid for the machinery £550
- Sold more goods on credit to B.Wilson £65
- Takings from cash sales were £350
- Bought another machine on credit from Armitage Ltd.£250.(Also for use in the business).

The first entry is one we've done before.

- Debit bank (in cash book)
- Credit capital account.

Bought office furniture by cheque should also be familiar:

- Credit bank
- Debit furniture account.

Bought machinery on credit here you must open an account for the supplier. You cannot put it through the cash book as you haven't paid yet. Instead of crediting the cash book you will credit the account for Armitage Ltd. The debit entry will be a Machinery account. Note that you open a machinery account as the machinery is for use in the business. If it had been for resale you could have entered it on the purchases account.

Cash sales entries are:
- Debit cash book (cash)
- Credit sales account.

Next Sally sold goods on credit to to B.Wilson. Again you cannot put this through the cash book as he hasn't yet paid. You will have to open an account for B.Wilson. You will debit the account for B.Wilson (instead of the cash book) and credit the sales account (just as you would for cash sales).

Paid for the machinery. The entries are:
- Credit cash book
- Debit Armitage Ltd.

The last three entries are really repeats so you should be able to work these out.

Fig 10.

Date	Details	Cash	Bank	Date	Details	Cash	Bank
	Capital		3600		Furniture		650
	Sales	58			Armitage		550
	Sales	350					
					To c/d	408	2400
		408	3600			408	3600
	B/d	408	2400				

Capital account

Date	Details	Debit	Credit	Balance
	Bank		3600	3600

Or the Capital account (and all the others) could be like this:-

	Debit	credit
		3600
To c/d	3600	
	3600	3600

b/d 3600

The first method (three column running balance) is the one you are more likely to be familiar with from bank statements. However, those are from the bank's point of view rather than yours, therefore cr and dr are opposite way round!

However, the second method is the one most often taught in classes, and you need to be aware of both methods.

Note that in the two column method, the amount to c/d is the amount needed to make the totals equal. (As in the cash book)

Furniture Account

Date	Details	Debit	Credit	Balance
	Bank	650		650

Armitage Account

Date	Details	Debit	Credit	Balance
	Inv		550	550cr
	Bank	550		0.00
	Inv		250	250cr

OR

It could be shown like this:

Debit	credit
	550
550	
	250
250 to cd	
750	750
	b/d 250

Machinery Account

Date	Details	Debit	Credit	Balance
	Armitage	550		550
	Armitage	250		800

Sales Account

Date	Details	Debit	Credit	Balance
	Cash		58	58cr
	B Wilson		72	130cr
	B Wilson		65	195cr
	Cash		350	545cr

B Wilson account

Date	Details	Debit	Credit	Balance
	Invoice	72		72
	Invoice	65		137

Note: In reality the date and invoice numbers would also be stated in the account.

The best way really to learn double entry book–keeping is by lots of practical experience. Therefore here are some more exercises to try. Keep your work carefully in a folder, as you will follow some of these accounts right through to working out their profit.

Mandy Baxter

Mandy Baxter decides to open a boutique. She:

- puts a £5500 cheque into a business bank account for the business.
- buys a second hand till for £60 cheque.
- then decides to take £100 out of the bank for cash for the till.
- buys some dress rails and display dummies for the shop (which she is renting.) She pays £1500 cheque.
- buys some new season's clothes on credit from Virgo Clothing Manufacturers for £2450.
- then pays her rent for the shop of £1200 by cheque.
- Her first week's trade is good and she takes £2350 in cash.
- She then decides to pay all but £100 of the cash into the bank.
- She pays Virgo Clothing Manufacturing the amount due to them.

Enter up all these accounts and balance off the cash book.

Check your answer (chapter 21) and, if correct, go on to the next one. If not, go through the correct answer slowly. The notes with the answers will help you.

Harry Webster

Oct 1   Harry put £5000 into a business bank account.
Oct 2   He bought a printing machine costing £2650 paying by cheque.

Oct 2   He also bought some paper and card (to print for resale). This was on credit £100 from Alpha Products.

Oct 3   Sold some printed sheets on credit to Balfyour Bell Ltd. £55.

Oct 4   He sold twenty printed leaflets to the Ladies Luncheon Club for £23 cash.

Oct 6   He sold more leaflets this time on credit to Silverman Insurance Brokers for £72.

Oct 7   He bought more paper from Alpha Products on credit for £75.

Oct 8   He paid Alpha Products £100 by cheque.

Oct 8   He sold some more printed tickets cash £50.

Write up the accounts.

CHECKLIST

1. What items are entered on the purchases Account?
2. What will the total of the sales Account tell you?
3. Which ledger contains assets, expenses and capital?

You can now look more closely at one of the ledgers.

THE SALES LEDGER

The **sales (debtors) ledger** contains the accounts of the people who owe you money.

If you were to go into a department store, buy a sweater, pay for it and walk out, that would be the end of that transaction. To the store this would count as a cash sale. If you were to go into a local builders' merchants and buy 3000 bricks and a ton of sand, you would probably ask them to send you a bill later. The builders' merchants would then have to open an account for you. They would record on that account the amount that these bricks and sand cost. They would also record on it anything else you may buy. This account would be in their sales ledger. This would probably be on a computer disc, but students find it easier to visualise the ledgers as sets of ledger cards. Each card is a customer's account. They are all kept in alphabetical order in a tray or box which supports them.

The entries for items the customer has bought, like the bricks and sand, are recorded as debits. A debit balance on a sales ledger account represents what the customer owes. The corresponding credit entry is on the sales account which is kept in the nominal ledger. That is how the book-keeper builds up the total sales figure.

When the customer pays any money towards this, it will be recorded in the cash book as a debit (remember the in and out sides) and the opposite (double) entry for this is credit the customer account. This, therefore, reduces the amount the customer owes. Note that the sales account is not affected by this. It remains as a record of total sales.

Any doubt as to whether an item is debit or credit can be solved by relating it back to the cash book.

The Sales Day Book

There are two ways of entering invoices (bills showing what the customers owe) on to the ledger. In the course of an average day there could be hundreds of invoices to enter. The text book way that invoices may be entered is via the sales day book. All invoices are written into this book first of all. This is why it is known as a book of original entry.

Fig.11. Sales Day Book

Date	Customer	Inv. No.	Goods Value	VAT	Total Invoice Value
29.09	P.Jones	123	50.00	8.75	58.75
30.09	B.Smith	124	100.00	17.50	117.50
Totals			150.00	26.25	176.25

Credit sales account   credit VAT account   posted to individual customer accounts as debits

You will see from the diagram of the sales Day Book in Figure 11 that the totals for the actual amount and the VAT are totalled separately. The total amount at the end is what will be entered each individual customer's account. The column showing the invoice total (minus VAT) will be totalled and this total will be entered on the credit of the sales account.

Similarly the VAT column will be totalled and entered to the credit of the VAT account. In this way you can see that the debit (to customer's account) equals the two credits to sales Account and VAT Account. The total of the other column can be entered on to the Control account.

Many firms use the following method. They first have someone pre–list the invoice totals. The accounts clerk may do this or perhaps a junior.

This means that the totals are added on a calculator which has a till roll, so that a written total is available and all the amounts are shown. Then the accounts clerk will enter all the invoices one by one using a computer keyboard.

When s/he has finished, the computer will give a total of all the invoices just entered. This should agree with the total on the pre–list. If it does, then that total is entered on to the Sales Ledger Control Account.

Payments are similarly entered, but from the cash book, using the cash book totals as a guide. The Control Account gives the total debtors figure. If the totals of all the sales ledger accounts are added, they should agree with the total on the control account.

Most computer packages will automatically enter the invoice total and the vat total on to the sales Account and VAT Account respectively. The clerk does not have to consider this.

At the end of every month, a copy of their account will be sent to each customer. This is known as the statement, and its purpose is to encourage the customer to pay the amount he owes.

When doing the exercises on double entry, you will have had more than one entry on your sales and purchases accounts. You can now see that the day book method would save time when entering by hand.

PURCHASE LEDGER

Note that the purchase (bought/creditors) ledger is entered in the same way, but with the entries the other way round. An invoice will be entered on an account in the purchase ledger as a credit. This is what you to the supplier. As far as you are concerned it is money going out. You can always relate to the cash book ins and outs. Remember that sales and purchase ledger accounts are just replacing the cash book entry until paid.

Just as you sent out statements to your customers, you will receive a copy of your account in their records from your suppliers. It is then the job of the purchase ledger clerk to ensure that this agrees with your records, before sending a payment to them.

Fig.12. Purchases Day Book
The purchase day book is almost identical to the sales day book.

Date	Supplier	Inv. No.	Goods Value	VAT	Total Invoice Value
01.10	J. Williams	632	42.00	7.35	49.35
02.10	B. Brocklesby	105	57.00	9.98	66.98
Totals			99.00	17.33	116.33
			Debit purchases account	Debit VAT account	Credit individual suppliers' accounts

An exercise using the day book method:

Mary Martin decides to open a printing business.

She:-

- begins by paying £6200 into a business bank account.
- Then buys printing equipment from Touchwood Enterprises Ltd for £2300 cheque
- Buys some paper (for printing on to) on credit from The Paper Path Co, for £200 plus VAT
- pays rent of £100 cheque.
- Sells some printed leaflets to A.South on credit for £50 plus VAT on credit
- She pays the window cleaner £5 in cash.

- Buys more paper from The Paper Path Co. for £75 plus £13.13 VAT.(on credit)
- Withdraws money for her own use £25 cash (called drawings).
- Sells 200 posters to A.South on credit for £45 plus VAT.

Returns

When goods are returned, or you return them, you do not enter then on the sales or purchases accounts. Instead you open special returns accounts. **Sales returns (returns inwards)** and **purchases returns (returns outwards).**

Mary also:-

- returns £25 (+ £4.38 VAT) worth of paper to The Paper Path Co, damaged.
- Sells 4 packets of cards to M.Sugden for £50 plus VAT on credit. M.Sugden returns one of these packets. (Show the last two separately.)
- She then sells 50 printed telephone pads for cash 62.60 plus 10.96 VAT.

An exercise for you to try

The following question is from the May 1989 GCSE exam of the London East Anglian Group.

J.Glendenning's purchases ledger contains the accounts of two creditors with the following balances :

	1988	£
August 1	J Haryott	500
	K Fellowes	670

During August the following transactions took place:

	1988	
Aug 1	J Haryott	500.00
	K. Fellowes	670.00

During August the following transactions took place:-

1988

August 4	Bought goods from J.Haryott on credit	1400.00
August 5	Purchases from J.Fellowes on credit	890.00
August 10	Returned damaged goods to K. Fellowes on credit	96.00
August 14	Sent J Haryott a cheque in settlement of her account at 1st August less 10 per cent cash discount	
August 19	Received a credit note from K.Fellowes for £40 in respect of an overcharge on 5th august.	
August 28th	J.Haryott complained that the discount deducted on 14 august should have been 5 per cent and asked for the error to be corrected.	

Prepare the accounts of J Haryott and K Fellowes as they would appear in J Glendenning's purchases ledger for the month of August 1988, bringing down each balance to 1 September 1988.

(Answer with others in back of book)

SUMMARY

- In debtors(sales) ledger the invoices are posted as debits and payments as credits.

- In creditors (purchase or bought) ledger invoices are posted as credits and payments as debits.

- Assets and expenses are debits (assets being things you own or are owed to you)

- Income and liabilities are credits (liabilities being what you owe)

- Purchases of assets are not entered on purchases account, but rather on an asset account (opened for the purpose if necessary).

3
Trial Balance

From time to time you will need to check the accuracy of your book-keeping. This must be done before preparation of the final accounts at the year end. However, it may be done at any time and many firms like it to be done every month before the statements go out to the customers, and payments are sent to the creditors. Alternatively it may be done half yearly, or at the end of the tax year. It really depends on company policy, and the time available.

HOW DO YOU DO A TRIAL BALANCE?

The way you check is to take out a **trial balance**. This is really very simple. It just means that you add up all the credit accounts, then all the debit accounts and the totals should be the same. For example, you entered all the accounts for John Moss in the last chapter. (Figures 7, 8 and 48). Now we will do his trial balance:

Trial Balance for John Moss as at ...(date)

	Dr	Cr
Cash	495	
Scales	150	
Capital		1000
Motor Van	500	
Purchases	600	
Sales		835
Rent	40	
Petrol	50	
	1835	1835

You can see that his credits and debits both add up to 1835, so it seems that you have entered his accounts correctly.

Now try to do Harry Webster's trial balance. (Answer in back of book)

If your trial balance totals do not agree, check the following :

Your arithmetic in totalling the balances.

Debits and credits are in correct columns.

You have copied the amounts correctly – it's a very common error to transpose figures eg 45 instead of 54.

You have not missed any accounts

Arithmetic in ledger accounts correct.

Author's Tip
When balancing any accounts, if the amount you are 'out' by is divisible by 9, then it is almost certain to be transposition of figures. eg. if the difference is 45 then you can work out that the figures involved are 27 written as 72 or vice versa (the difference between these two figures being 45).

USING SUSPENSE ACCOUNTS
Sometimes, in spite of all your efforts, you just cannot find the error(s) which are causing your trial balance to disagree. You cannot allow your accounts to disagree, but you cannot afford to spend any more time looking for the error(s). There is a solution to the problem. You open a suspense account. This is an account which you make up. It holds the difference in your trial balance totals. For example:

Trial Balance

	Dr	Cr
Cash	25000	
Bank	20000	
Capital		40000
Debtors	10000	
Creditors		12000
Sales		47960
Purchases	45000	
	100000	99960
Suspense account		40
	100000	100000

The amount of the suspense account makes the trial balance agree. If you subsequently find an error, you must correct it using the suspense account as the other half of the entry. eg Suppose, in the previous example, the error was found to be a cheque received, and entered in the cash book, from B Jackson for £440. It had been credited to B.Jackson's account as $400. To correct this error, you now have to debit the suspense account £40 and credit B Jackson £40. This will put things right.

Journal Entries

You need to make a record of this, so that at a later date, perhaps when the books are being audited (checked by an independent accountant), it will be easy for anyone to see what you did. The place you record this is in the Journal. The Journal is just a record of events. It is not an account, nor part of the double entry system. The error you have just corrected would be shown in the journal with an explanation.

Fig 13. Recording in the Journal

		Dr	Cr
6 Nov	Suspense Account	40.00	
	B. Jackson		40.00
	Being correction of cheque posted as incorrect amount.		

The explanation is called the narrative, and traditionally begins with he word 'being.' These days it is acceptable to just state the reason for the entry without the 'being.'

ERRORS NOT SHOWN BY TRIAL BALANCE

By now you are beginning to realise that there always have to be snags with accounts. Unfortunately, the trial balance has its drawbacks. Various errors could occur in the accounts which would *not* show up in the trial balance.

Many students find this confusing at first. It must be stressed that the following list of types of error *would not be shown up by the trial balance.*

1. Commission (Misposting):
Entered on the right side of the right type of account, but the wrong one eg. Rent instead of rates, or perhaps B.Wilson instead of G.Wilson.

2. Principle:
Entered on right side of wrong type of account. eg. Purchase of an asset entered on purchase account instead of asset account. (Remember John Moss's purchase of van).

3. Omission:
Item completely omitted from everywhere

4. Compensating:
An error has been made on both dr and cr which compensate so that trial balance totals still agree. eg. Suppose an account has been debited with 150 should be 200. Then another account has been credited with 350 which should be 400. You will be 50 short on the dr side, but also 50 short on the cr side so totals will still agree.

5. Reversal of entries:
The entries have been made the wrong way round. eg Cash sales entered as cr cash book dr sales account (when of course it should be vice versa.)

6. Original entry:
The wrong figure used throughout, but all entries otherwise correct. eg. A cheque received from a customer for £55 has been entered as dr cash book £50 and cr customer account £50. (dr and cr correct – amount wrong.)

Spotting the types of error in the trial balance

The above types of error must be learned and understood as the GCSE exams always contain some sort of question(s) on them. You are often asked to give examples, so you may like to think of some of your own too, checking to make sure they do not make the trial balance disagree.

Try the following

State what type of error is involved in the examples below:

B.Snaith bought goods from M.G.Mason on credit for £36. This transaction was entered as a credit on the account of G.M.Mason.

A credit sale of £300 was entered in double entry accounts as £30

A purchase of £250 was entirely omitted from the books.

When B.Smith paid the £50 he owed to us, you debited his account and credited the cash book.

When you paid £500 rent, this was entered onto the debit side of an account in the purchase ledger.

When a customer paid us £35, you debited the cash book but also debited his account with the £35. In the same period you debited an invoice from a supplier for £35 to the supplier's account in the purchase ledger.

If errors are discovered after preparation of final accounts, then it will be necessary to correct these also. Later in the book you will find worked examples involving the correction of errors in conjunction with corrected net profit figures.

Another exercise for you to try:
Try this extract from an exam question (NEA 1989)
(ignore the part which mentions balance sheet)

What is a Trial Balance ?
What is the purpose of a Trial Balance ?
How does a Trial Balance differ from a Balance Sheet?
Name four types of error which will <u>not</u> be revealed by a Trial Balance.

Using *two* of your types of error as above, explain why they *will not* be revealed by a Trial Balance.

Write down *four* different examples of errors which could have been made in the books of account, and would result in the in the Trial Balance totals not being equal.

Explain the reasons why each of the following steps may be taken to try to trace the error when a Trial Balance does *not* balance.

Check any transaction with a value equal to the difference between the Trial Balance totals.

Check any transaction with a value equal to half the difference between the trial balance totals.

4
Trading and Profit and Loss Accounts

Working out profit is not as straightforward as you may think. Suppose you bought 372 books at £3.50 each, then sold 129 books at £4.75 each. How much profit will you have made ?

Bought 372 at £3.50 each = 1302

Sold 129 at £4.75 each = 612.75

The simplest answer would be 689.25 (1302 – 612.75), but this would be wrong. It is necessary to take into account the books (stock) you have left.

Another way to work it out would be 129 X £1.25 (difference) = 161.25

That is the correct answer, but the way accountants work it out is:

Sales less cost of sales.

The formula for cost of sales is:
Opening stock (Stock you have to start with)
plus purchases (of stock)
less closing stock (stock you have left).

To work out the stock figures you use the cost price of the stock. The only exception to this would be if the selling price was lower– obsolete/deteriorated stock sold off cheaply.

Sales		612.75
Less cost of sales		
No opening stock		
Purchases	1302.00	
Less closing stock (243 x 3.50)	850.00	
		451.50
Gross profit		161.25

This is called a trading account, and is usually done at the year end. The title is very important. It is Trading Account for the year ended (giving the date) and also gives the name of the trader.

SUMMARY OF TRADING ACCOUNTS

- The title includes the words 'for the year ended.'

- Opening stock will only occur if previous trading has taken place

- Stock is valued at cost price (or selling price if this is lower)

- Total obtained is the <u>Gross</u> profit

You value the stock at the lower of cost or sale price because of another accounting concept. This is the prudence(conservatism) concept. This is that you must never overstate profit (or over value an asset). You must always be cautious, even pessimistic.

A Sample Trading Account

Now try doing John Moss's Trading account assuming he had £50 worth of saleable root vegetables left.
You should have a gross profit of £285

To take it further you must deduct expenses. It will then be known as a trading and profit & loss account. After deducting the expenses you will arrive at the net profit.

John had expenses of Rent £20 X 2 and Petrol £50. Note that the van and scales are not included here. They are assets. The expenses you want are just the day to day running expenses.

So John's Trading and Profit & Loss account will look like this:

Trading and Profit & Loss Account for John Moss for the year ended …(date)

Sales		835.00
Less cost of sales :		
No opening stock		
Purchases	600.00	
Less closing stock	50.00	
	———	
		550.00
		———
Gross profit		285.00
Less expenses:		
Rent	40.00	
Petrol	50.00	
	———	
		90.00
		———
Net profit		195.00

MAKING ADJUSTMENTS

Sometimes, certain adjustments have to be made to the figures used in the Trading and Profit & Loss Account. Occasionally, when people, or other firms, buy goods they return them for one reason or another. Goods returned to us are known as returns inwards or sales returns. If you return goods they are known as returns outwards or purchase returns.

The Sales returns must be deducted from the sales figure before working out the gross profit.

The purchase returns must similarly be deducted from the purchases figure. e.g. Suppose a trader sold £50 worth of goods, then a customer returned an item worth £5. This same trader bought goods for £30, but sent back items to the value of £10. He had £7 worth of stock left. His trading account would look like this :

Sales	50.00
Less returns inward	5.00

		45.00
Purchases	30.00	
Less returns outward	10.00	
	20.00	
Less closing stock	7.00	
Cost of sales		13.00
Gross profit		32.00

There are other adjustments which may have to be made. When you buy goods, you often have to pay carriage and/or packing costs. These will have to be added to the purchases figure. Note, however, that carriage on sales is <u>never</u> shown in the trading account. All selling and distribution expenses are shown further down in the profit and loss section, under expenses. If there are warehousing costs, these are also added to the purchases figure.

SUMMARY OF ADJUSTMENTS
Returns inwards (sales returns) are deducted from sales.
Returns outwards (purchase returns) are deducted from purchases.
Carriage inwards is added to purchases
Carriage outwards is shown under expenses in the profit and loss section.
Always use labels ie cost of sales, gross profit and net profit.

If there was any interest received, or dividends from investments etc. this would be *added on* after expenses. If there was any interest payable or similar charges, then this would be deducted. In that order.

Some Exercises

Now practise some trading and profit and loss accounts. Some of them are questions from past exam papers and this is indicated. Don't forget the correct title – for the year ended etc.

B.Burton's figures at the year end were:

Purchase	4850
Sales	1000
Stock at beg. of year	2950
Stock at end of year	3270
Electricity	500
Travelling expenses	420
Administration expenses	310

Write up his Trading and Profit and Loss Account for the year.

N.Iveson's Trial Balance was as follows:

	Dr	Cr
Motor Vehicle	1800	
Furniture and fittings	14000	
Capital		3000
Sales		15000
Purchases	21000	
Debtors and creditors	9500	8300
Stock	4500	
Expensees	500	
Bank	2000	
	53300	53300

Write up his Trading and Profit and Loss Account, using the figures you require. His closing stock was £3200.

N.Carter's Account

After his first year of trading, Nathan Carter produced these figures:

Opening Stock	10000
Closing Stock	14000
Sales	25713
Purchases	19642

Returns inwards	235
Carriage inwards	242
Returns outwards	150
Salaries	4214
Capital	12000
Administration exp.	2231
Rent	3210

Write up his Trading and Profit and Loss Account.

Exercise:

This question is from the London East Anglia Group exam paper May 1989.

The following information for J.Baker relates to the final quarter of 1988. Prepare the trading and profit and loss account for this period.

	£
Stock at start	5000
Stock at close	4500
Purchases	25000
Sales	37000
Returns inwards	250
Carriage inwards	750
Carriage outwards	1050
Wages (trading account)	9500
Selling expenses	750
Returns outwards	900

Note that although wages are normally deducted in the Profit and Loss section, here you are told specifically to deduct them in Trading Account.

CORRECTED NET PROFIT

As stated in the last chapter, sometimes errors are discovered which were not shown up by the trial balance. This means that you will have prepared our trading and profit and loss account, so you will have to do a corrected net profit calculation.

Suppose Joe's Fish Shop Net Profit was £1500.
Then he found that his closing stock figure was £500 and not £445 as he had first thought. Also his purchases had been £155 more than the figure he had used.

The corrected net profit is calculated like this:

Net profit	1500
Add adjustment to closing stock	55
	1555
Less adjustment to purchases figure	155
Corrected net profit	1400

The closing stock adjustment is added because the closing stock figure used had been lower. Had it been the true value, there would have been more to deduct from opening stock + purchases. Therefore a lower figure would have been taken from sales to arrive at a greater profit.

Similarly, had his purchases figure been greater (as it should have been) then there would have been a greater figure to deduct from sales making the profit figure lower.

To convince yourself of this, try a simple trading account like this :

Sales		6
Opening stock	5	
+ Purchases	3	
	8	
– closing stock	4	
		4
		2

Now suppose his closing stock was 5 not 4.
There would be 3 to take from the 6, so profit would be 3 not 2.

Now suppose that his purchases had been 4 not 3. You can work that through and see that it would reduce the profit.

PROFIT ADJUSTMENTS
Try the following :

If purchases were overvalued how would this affect gross profit?
If a gas bill of £434 has been paid, but entered in the books as £334, how would this affect the Net Profit ?
If stock at the end of a period is undervalued, would this increase or decrease Gross Profit ?
Suppose an item of £252 rent paid had been entered in the cash book, but the other half of the double entry not done, how would this affect the Net Profit ?

This is part of an exam question from the NEA Board 1989 exam. The other part was used in the previous section.

After the draft final accounts for the year ended 30 April 1989 had been prepared, the following errors were discovered.

Drawings of £400 had been entered in the Profit and Loss Account on the debit side. (Answer: +400)
Stock at 30 April 1989 had been overvalued by £620.
The total of the Purchases Day Book had been over–added by £680.
Returns outwards of £5000 had been deducted from the sales.
The Provision for Doubtful Debts had not been increased from £900 to £1200.
No adjustment had been made for advertising prepaid of £400.

For *each* of these errors in turn show how the net profit would be affected *after* the error is corrected. In each case indicate whether the net profit would increase (+) or decrease (–) and by how much. Number 1 has been completed as an example.

PREPAYMENTS AND ACCRUALS
When you prepare the profit and loss account, you only want to include expenses pertaining to *that year*. This means that any prepaid expenses i.e. paid in advance for next year, will have to included in next year's accounts and not in this year's.

However, any accrued expenses i.e. still owing at the end of the year, will have to be included in this years's account, as they have been incurred this year.

It often happens that amounts are split, because a firm's financial year may not agree with the times for paying bills. For instance, suppose you started a business and paid a year's rent in advance on 1 April. Our financial year is going to be the calendar year (You will do our final accounts to 31 Dec). This means that you will have paid three months (Jan–March) which you will not want to include in our accounts for the year ending 31 Dec. That will be a prepayment. You will have to <u>deduct</u> that amount from our figure for he profit and loss account.

Suppose you rent machinery and pay the rent quarterly, two weeks after the end of each quarter. On 31 Dec you will be owing the rent for that quarter (Oct–Dec). You will have to <u>include</u> that rental in our accounts as it applies to this year.

As the profit and loss is an account, then the amounts are taken from the expense accounts to post to it eg electricity – suppose you have worked out that the four quarters for this year amounted to £500 (perhaps this isn't what is on the account), then you will credit the electricity account with £500 and debit the profit and loss account £500.This way the adjustments are taken care of every year, and only that year's amount is posted to the profit and loss account.

SUMMARY OF PREPAYMENTS AND ACCRUALS
It is the time when debts are incurred that is important – not when payment is made.
The profit and loss account includes everything pertaining to that year whether paid or not.

Try the following which includes prepayment and accrual.

N.Barlow has a list of figures with which to work out his final accounts.

Sales	23000
Purchases	15000
Opening Stock	7500
Closing stock	5500
Insurance	800
Electricity	650
Administration expenses	2300
Wages and Salaries	16000

£200 of the insurance was paid in advance for next year, but £150 of the electricity had been owing (accrued) from last year.

Write up his Trading and Profit and Loss Account.

5
The Balance Sheet

The next stage is to prepare the balance sheet. The balance sheet really is a list of assets and liabilities, showing how they were financed. Whereas, the trading and profit and loss account is for the year ended, the balance sheet is the state of affairs as at a particular date. This is because the balance sheet is not an account like the profit and loss. It doesn't cover a period of time, it merely shows how things are at that date.

The correct title is Balance sheet for (name) as at (date). Begin by listing the assets.

WHAT ARE ASSETS ?
There are different types of asset. The main ones are fixed and current.

Fixed Assets
These are items owned by the business , and which are regarded as fairly permanent. eg The premises, fixtures and fittings in the premises, motor vehicles, machinery, equipment and so on.

Current Assets
These are the fluctuating assets – stock, debtors, bank and cash. They are listed in order of liquidity with least liquid first. Liquid, in the accounting sense, means transferrable into cash. Current assets are all liquid assets in that they are frequently being converted, directly or indirectly, into cash. They are constantly on the move. If you think of current as being the current of a fast flowing river this may help you to remember what current assets are.

Current liabilities
The next thing you do is to list the current liabilities. Liabilities are items owed by you. Therefore the creditors figure is a liability. Strictly speaking, a current liability is a debt which falls due within one year, so a long term loan is not a current liability. However, a bank overdraft can be called in by the bank at any time, and is therefore a current liability.

Working capital

The current liabilities are deducted from the <u>current</u> assets to give what is known as the 'Working Capital.' This is a very important figure.
The working capital is then added to the fixed assets. The resulting total is the Net Assets.

Long-Term Liability
Any long term liabilities are labelled as such, and deducted from net assets total. The final total is then known as net worth.

Financed by
You then have to say how the assets are financed, so you list the capital, long term loans, net profit and deduct any drawings. Drawings are money taken out of the business by the owner for his own use. The total should be the same as for net assets. Look at the example of John Moss's Balance sheet.

Balance Sheet for John Moss as at ...(date)

Fixed Assets
Motor Van   500
Scales   <u>150</u>
                                             650

Current Assets
Stock   50
Cash   <u>495</u>
                                    545
Current Liabilities   <u>0</u>
                                             <u>545</u>
Net Worth   <u>1195</u>
Financed by:
Capital at start   1000
 Add net profit   <u>195</u>
                                             <u>1195</u>

SUMMARY
The title must always include the words 'as at.'
Always use the correct labels for totals ie working capital, net assets.

Draw up a Balance Sheet
From the following figures, draw up the balance sheet of B.Bertram as at 31 Dec :–

Premises	28,000
Van	5,000
Stock	4,000
Bank	1,000
Debtors	2,500
Creditors	3,000
Capital	30,000
Net Profit	8,000
Drawings	500

Do not look at the answer until you have made a good attempt. This will be to your advantage – practise is the key to success with accounts.
If you've got that right, try the next one for revision of profit and loss accounts also.

G.Cooper's balances at 31 Dec :–

Premises	30,000	
Fittings	5,000	
Insurance	500	(an expense)
Van	6,500	
Sales	40,000	
Wages	5,000	
Debtors	7,000	
Purchases	30,000	
Closing stock	10,000	
Capital	59,000	
Creditors	4,000	
Rates	3,000	
Electricity	2,000	
Bank	10,000	
Drawings	4,000	

Now that you are doing balance sheets as well as profit and loss accounts, you may sometimes wonder in which of these a particular item goes. This is why there is a prompt in brackets beside insurance. So that you can work it out for yourself without any prompting you will have to study the following explanation.

Revenue expenditure goes in the profit and loss account.
Capital expenditure goes in the balance sheet.

Revenue expenditure
Revenue expenses are those incurred in the day to day running of the business such as salaries, electricity, insurance, purchase of goods for resale, maintenance etc.

Capital expenditure
This is the purchase of fixed assets which will not be consumed during the accounting period (usually one year). eg purchase of new vehicles, fixtures and fittings, machinery etc. These are permanent in accounting terms – will still be present next year.
However, small inexpensive items such as staplers are counted as revenue expenses and shown in the profit and loss account.
It is very important to be able to distinguish between capital and revenue expenses as they have a direct effect on the profit figures. If you were to buy a new van, and charge it to profit and loss account, it could have a disastrous effect on this year's profit. The balance sheet would not show it as an asset, so that would be inaccurate too.

Sometimes the profit and loss account is called a revenue statement. Perhaps this will help you to remember where revenue expenses go.

EXERCISES IN BALANCE SHEETS
Try this balance sheet from the NEA 1989 Summer exam :

The following balances remained in the books of Jason Green, a sole trader, after the preparation of the Trading and Profit and Loss Accounts for the year ended 31 May 1989 .

	£
Capital (1 June 1988)	89000
Drawings	6000

Expense creditors	580
Trade debtors	4000
Fixtures and fittings	12000
Expenses prepaid	800
Trade creditors	2000
Mortgage on premises	6000
Cash balance	200
Bank overdraft	1420
Net loss for the year ended 31 May 1989	1000
Premises	60000
Stock (31 May 1989)	15000

Set out the Balance Sheet of Jason Green as at 31 May, showing clearly the totals of the following :

fixed assets
current assets
current liabilities
long term liabilities
working capital
net assets

6
Accounting for Depreciation

One revenue expense not yet mentioned is depreciation. Assets wear out, or become less valuable with time. We all know that a new car is worth a lot less as soon as it has been bought, even when it has only been driven to the end of the street! It is no longer brand new. Each year it will be worth less. The same lessening of value happens with other assets, though not usually land or premises. However, a quarry or mine may be worth less as it begins to run short of its product.

It is sensible to account for this in the balance sheet, and profit and loss account, year by year. Otherwise you would have accounts showing that you own a lot in assets. This would go against the Accounting principle of Prudence (conservatism). The assets would be over stated. Therefore, accountants spread the depreciation over the life of the asset. This depreciation is set against the profit in the profit and loss account as an expense.

It is rather like saying that your car costs you £20 a week overall, and not just the £5 worth of petrol you put in it. It may work out at an average of £5 a week to cover servicing/maintenance. The £20 includes £10 to cover the wear and tear (depreciation) as well. A brand new car would cost more in depreciation to begin with, but you may wish to spread this cost over its life. You could work this out using the straight line method of depreciation. This is one of three methods of calculating depreciation.

THE STRAIGHT LINE METHOD

The formula for straight line is :

Cost less scrap value
Useful life in years

Suppose you buy a car for £3500 and hope to get £500 for it in three years time.

$$\frac{3500-500}{3} = 1000$$

You would have to depreciate the car by £1000 per year. If you thought it may last six years, then you would have to depreciate by £500 a year which is close to the £10 per week mentioned above.

Alternatively, this may have been worked out for you and you may be given a percentage figure. If you are told to depreciate 10% per year by the straight line method, this means that you depreciate 10% of the original figure each year.
eg Van costing £6000 to be depreciated at 10% straight line:

1st year depreciation £600
2nd year depreciation £600

It will be the same each year.

THE REVALUATION METHOD

A second method is simply to revalue everything every year. The depreciation is the difference between last years value and this years. For example:

1st year asset worth £8000
2nd year valued at £7500 so depreciation = £500
3rd year valued at £6100 so depreciation = £1400

This is commonly used where lots of small tools, which are frequently replaced, are kept. An estimate of the value of them as a whole is used. It sounds like a very exact method, but requires an expert valuation each year. The other two methods can be worked out by the accounts department without calling anyone else in.

REDUCING (DIMINISHING) BALANCE

A third method is to charge a percentage each year on the reducing balance.
This differs from the straight line percentage in that you are taking the percentage of a different figure each year.
For instance, the van costing £6000 is to be depreciated at 10% using the reducing balance method:

1st year depreciation = £600
2nd year depreciation = (10% of £6000–600) = £540
3rd year depreciation = (10% of £5400–540) = £486, and so on.

This is the method used by HM Customs and Revenue to calculate Capital Allowances (their term for depreciation).

USING THE DIFFERENT METHODS

Whichever of these methods is chosen, it must be the one used every year. This is in accordance with the Consistency concept of accounting. You will see, after working out some examples. that each method gives a different result. If an accountant used a different method from one year to the next, a comparison of his final accounts would not be a fair comparison. It would be possible to change the method just before a proposed sell out of the business, in order to make it look more profitable. When you have worked the following exercises, you may like to try to do them again using a different method. Of course you cannot use revaluation for this.

Try working with each method

Straight Line
Car cost £12000, eight years life, sale value £400

Reducing balance
Calculate for first three years:
Van cost £10000. Depreciate at 15% per year (round up to nearest pound)

Revaluation
Cost of tools first year = £250
Valued second year at £215
Depreciation = ?

DEPRECIATION IN FINAL ACCOUNTS

Depreciation is treated as a revenue expense. It is therefore deducted from the profit in the profit and loss account along with all the other expenses. It also reduces the value of fixed assets and must be accounted for in the balance sheet too.

Look at the accounts of G.Cooper which you did in the chapter on balance sheets.

Suppose that the fittings were depreciated by 10% straight line, and the van by 20% straight line.

The expenses in the profit and loss account will now include £500 depreciation on fittings and £1300 depreciation on van.

Profit and Loss Account for G.Cooper for the year ended..(date)

Sales		40000
Purchases	30000	
–Closing stock	10000	
Cost of sales		20000
Gross profit		20000
Insurance	500	
Wages	5000	
Rates	3000	
Electricity	2000	
Depreciation:		
Van	1300	
Fittings	500	
		12300
Net profit		7700

Balance Sheet for G.Cooper as at ....(date)

Fixed Assets	Cost	Accumulated Depreciation	Net
Premises	30000	-	30000
Fittings	5000	500	4500
Van	6500	1300	5200
	41500	1800	39700
Current Assets			
Stock	10000		
Debtors	7000		
Bank	10000		
		27000	
Current Liabilities			
Creditors		4000	-
			23000
			62700
Financed by:			
`Capital at start	59000		
Add net profit	7700		
		66700	
Less drawings		4000	
			62700

Fig 14. Balance sheet showing depreciation

Notice that the balance sheet has special columns for depreciation, as shown in Fig. 14.

In the second year the depreciation will include both years' depreciation. (This only applies to the balance sheet– remember that the profit and loss account contains only items pertaining to that year.)

Balance sheet extract from the following year:

	cost	accumulated depreciation	net
Fixed Assets			
Premises	30,000	–	30,000
Fittings	5,000	1,000	4,000
Van	6,500	2,600	3,900
	41,500	3,600	37,900

Note that the cost and depreciation columns are ruled off under the totals, and not added in.

SUMMARY OF THE DIFFERENT METHODS

With the straight line method the depreciation is the same each year
Only that year's depreciation is entered in the profit and loss account
The accumulated depreciation is shown in the balance sheet.

BOOK KEEPING FOR DEPRECIATION

There are two ways of entering depreciation in our book keeping system. One way is just to keep entering the depreciation on the asset account. For instance, in the example above, G.Cooper could enter depreciation on his van account, as shown below:

Van Account

	Dr	Cr	Bal
Bank	6500		6500
Yr 1 Depreciation		1300	5200
Yr 2 Depreciation		1300	3900

Fig. 15. Entering depreciation on the asset account

Provision for Depreciation Account

Another way to do it is to have a separate account for depreciation. This way the van account can still show the cost of the van. This extra account will be called the provision for depreciation account. It will show the accumulated depreciation on the van.

The word provision is misleading. It would be better if the account was called the accumulated depreciation account. It in no way provides anything. It is not to replace assets. It is merely to avoid overstating the value of assets.

Depreciation Account

In addition to this, you have to open a depreciation account. This will show just the years depreciation which will be transferred to the profit and loss account each year. Therefore the account will never have more than that years depreciation on it.

Fig. 16. Provision for depreciation on a van. There would also be depreciation on fittings or any other depreciating assets on the last account.

Provision for depreciation on Van

	Dr	Cr	Bal
1st Year (date)		1300	1300
2nd Year (date)		1300	2600cr

Van Account

	Dr	Cr	Bal
Date Bank	6500		6500

Depreciation Account

	Dr	Cr	Bal
1st Year (date)	1300		1300
Profit and Loss a/c		1300	0
2nd Year (date)	1300		1300
Profit and loss a/c		1300	0

This may seem confusing, but just remember that the provision account is the one with the amount for the balance sheet. The depreciation account is the one with the balance for profit and loss account. If you are writing up your own accounts you might well decide simply to depreciate on the asset account, but then you will have to work out the amounts for each of the final accounts.

Now try these :–

Z & G Castings Account
Write up the provision for depreciation account for Z and G Castings for the first three years:

They bought a machine for £3000,
They depreciated it by 20% per year on the reducing balance.

Also show how the entries would appear in the balance sheet for the three years (short extract only)

AB Engineering.
They bought a machine for £20,000.
Depreciate at 10% straight line for the first three years.

Show the balance sheet extract for each year. How much will appear in the profit and loss account each year ?

DISPOSAL ACCOUNTS

There is a special way of accounting for the sale of assets. It is simply that you open a disposal account, and transfer everything pertaining to the asset on to this account. Suppose AB Engineering were to sell their machine at the end of the three years for £10500.

They would first credit the machine account and then open a disposal account, debiting the amount to it.

Then they would debit the provision for depreciation account, and credit this amount to the disposal account.

Then when they got the money for the machine, they would debit the cash book and credit the disposal account.

Whatever amount is left on the disposal account will be transferred to the profit and loss account that year. (See Figure 17.)

If AB Engineering had sold the machine for £15,000 however, the amount to transfer to the profit and loss account would be a credit. They would have made a profit on the sale, so the amount would be credited (added to) the profit and loss account rather than debited (deducted like expenses).

Disposal Account

	Dr	Cr	Bal
(From) Machine Account (you will credit machine account and debit this account)	20000		20000
Provision for depreciation account (You will debit the provision for dep.account and credit this account)		6000	14000
Bank (Dr. Bank Cr this account)		10500	3500
Profit and Loss account (Cr this account and Dr profit and loss account)		3500	0

Fig. 17. A Disposal account with explanations of the entire double entry. The explanations are for the benefit of the student and would not normally appear in the account. Only the handwritten items would appear.

7
Bad Debts

The sales ledger is always bound to show accounts which will never be paid. Some customers will have gone bankrupt; perhaps some dispute their account and so on. Some of these debts are not worth spending money to recover. You don't want to show, in your final accounts, year after year that you have a current asset (debtors) of a certain sum if this is not recoverable. This would not be in line with the Prudence (Conservatism) concept of accounting. Of course this means that the book keeping is going to be even more complicated.

If you decide to write off a debt altogether you must deduct it from the profit in the profit and loss account. Supposing you are quite certain that G.Glover will never pay you the £50 he owes, you have to write it off in two steps.

BAD DEBTS ACCOUNT

The first thing to do is to open a bad debts account. Then transfer the debt to it by crediting G.Glover account £50 and debiting the bad debt account £50. This has cleared Glover's account and transferred the debt to the bad debt account.

At the end of the year you have to transfer the debt to the profit and loss account. By this time, there may have been other amounts entered on the bad debts account. The bad debts account is credited for the amount on it, and this same amount is debited to the profit and loss account.

Suppose that the £50 was the only amount that year. The bad debts account would be credited with £50 and the profit and loss account would be debited with the £50.

The bad debts account holds the debts until they are written off to the profit and loss account. Therefore this account will reduce to nil each year end.

PROVISION FOR BAD DEBTS

A prudent accountant should provide for the possibility of bad debts, rather than wait for them to have to be written off. This is because he will otherwise be overstating the profits and worth of the business. If say 7% of our debts are doubtful, then you will be overstating the worth of the business by that 7%. To provide for the doubtful debts, you open a **provision for bad (doubtful) debts** account.

You have to decide what percentage of your debtors will not pay. Suppose you have a total debtors figure of £5000, and decide to provide for 5% bad debts.

The provision account will show a credit of £250.

The double entry is:

- credit provision for bad debts account
- debit profit and loss account.

Suppose in year two our total debtors figure is £6000. You will need to have a provision of £300. The provision account already shows £250 so only £50 need to be debited to the profit and loss account.

Provision for Bad Debts Account

	Dr	Cr	Bal
1st Year		250.00	250cr
(you will debit the profit and loss account)			
2nd Year		50.00	300cr
(debit P & L Account)			

Fig. 18. Debiting Provision for Bad Debts

Suppose that in the third year the debtors figure is only £4000. The provision needed is £200. That year £100 will be <u>credited</u> to the profit and loss account.

	Dr	Cr	Bal
1st Year		250.00	250cr
(you will debit the profit and loss account)			
2nd Year		50.00	300cr
(debit P & L Account)			
3rd Year (credit Proft and loss a/c)	100		200cr

Fig. 19. Crediting Provision for Bad Debts

Treatment in the balance sheet

Each year, the provision must be deducted from the debtors figure in the balance sheet. Using the above example, in year one £250 would have been deducted, in year two £300 and in year three £200.

Fig 20. Bad debts provision in the balance sheet.
Balance Sheet Extract for each of the three years:

1st Year

<u>Current Assets</u>

Debtors	5000.00	
Less provision for bad debts	<u>250.00</u>	
	4750.00	

2nd Year

<u>Current Assets</u>

Debtors	6000.00	
Less provision for bad debts	<u>300.00</u>	
	5700.00	

3rd Year

Current Assets
Debtors   4000.00
Less provision for bad debts   200.00
                                 3800.00

SUMMARY

- Bad Debts account is only for accounts actually written off.
- Provision for Bad Debts appears in the balance sheet as a direct percentage of that year's debtors.
- The provision appears in the profit and loss account as the amount needed to bring the provision account to its correct total.
- The balance on the provision account should be the percentage required of that year's debtors.

Now try some exercises :

B.Taggart's debtors

B.Taggart has a total debtors figure of £5750. He finds that he will have to write off £750. He would like to provide 7% for bad debts on the remainder of his debtors.

Write up the bad debts account, provision for bad debts account, and show balance sheet extracts, and the amounts which will be entered in the profit and loss accounts.

M Bedwin's debtors

M.Bedwin had debtors of £3630 in 1988, £4720 in 1989 and £5940 in 1990. Write up the [provision for bad debts (5% per year). Also show the amounts which would appear in the profit and loss account and show balance sheet extracts for the three years

M.Cox's debtors

M.Cox had debtors of £3226 in 1988, £5240 in 1989 and £5620 in 1990.

In 1989 he wrote off £326 in bad debts. After doing this he decided to provide for 10% bad debts from 1989 onwards.

Write up all his accounts as for previous question.

8
Manufacturing Accounts

Some businesses don't just buy things and then sell them again. They buy in raw materials, make these into something else, then sell them. These businesses have to prepare an extra account, before the profit and loss account. It is called a **manufacturing account**.

PRIME COST

The first part of the account deals with **prime costs**. Prime costs are any costs which are directly involved in the manufacture of the goods. eg raw materials, wages of assembly workers. Another direct cost is **royalties**. This is the amount paid to the patent holder for each item produced. As it relates exactly to each item, it is directly attributable to manufacture, and so is a direct cost.

PRODUCTION COST

The other, indirect, costs are called **production costs**. These include things like repairs to machinery and wages of factory nurse. Although necessary for production they are not directly concerned with the finished product.

WORKING OUT THE TYPES OF COST

Study the following list and see if you can decide which are prime and which are production costs :

- Haulage costs bringing raw materials
- Wages of machine operators in factory
- Cost of raw materials
- Repairs to machinery
- Wages of maintenance staff in factory
- Salary of factory nurse
- Wages of assembly workers
- Insurance for factory
- Oil for factory machines
- Depreciation of factory machinery

An Example

The following figures are for G.Gladwin Ltd:

Stock of raw materials in Jan	500
Stock of raw materials in Dec(same year)	700
Purchases of raw materials	8000
Direct wages	21000
Factory Rent(not including offices)	440
Royalties	150
Depreciation on factory machinery	400
Indirect wages	9000
General factory expenses (indirect)	310

The account will be laid out like this :

Manufacturing Account for G.Gladwin for the year ended...(date)

Stock of raw materials in Jan	500	
+ Purchases	8000	
		8500
Less stock of raw materials Dec		700
Cost of raw materials consumed		**7800**
Direct wages	21000	
Royalties	150	
		21150
Prime Cost		**28950**

Factory Overheads:-		
Rent	440	
Indirect wages	9000	
Indirect expenses	310	
Depreciation	400	
	————	
		10150
		————
Production Cost of completed goods		**39100**

Note the labels of the totals throughout the account – cost of raw materials consumed, prime cost and production cost of finished goods. It is very important to use these labels. In any exam question you may well be asked to show them, in which case it would be a good idea to underline your wording for them. In the example of G.Gladwin they have been shown in bold text, as have their corresponding totals.

SUMMARY

- Prime costs are the direct costs
- Production costs are the indirect costs
- Always use labels of totals

A Manufacturing Account

Now try the following manufacturing account:

Stock of raw materials at start	650
Stock of raw materials at end	700
Purchases of raw materials	1000
Factory rent	900
Depreciation of machinery	400
Direct wages	3000
Maintenance wages	2000
Royalties	300
Parts for machine repairs	100

WORK IN PROGRESS

In the factory, at any given time, there will not just be finished goods at one end and the raw materials at the other. There are bound to be half finished goods somewhere along the line. These half finished goods are called **work in progress**. When working out the production cost, you have to take them into account. They are obviously worth something. The way to account for them is very simple. You just add **work in progress at start** and take off **work in progress at end**. This will give us the value of work in progress during the period. You don't have to worry about working out the value of the work in progress at start and end. This will have been done for you.

Suppose G.Gladwin had £13,200 work in progress at start and £13,000 at end. This would appear like this in his account:

Production cost	39100
Add work in progress at start	13200
	52300
Less work in progress at end	13000
Production cost of completed goods	39300

The next thing you need to know is how to progress from this account to the trading and profit and loss account. A lot of students seem to forget this part so it's a good idea to pay particular attention to it.

Suppose Gladwin has the following figures in addition to the above:

Sales	62,000
Opening stock of finished goods	17,500
Closing stock of finished goods	13,750
Salaries of Office Staff	5,000
Commission of Salesmen	6,500
Tax and Insurance for delivery van	400

His trading and profit and loss account would look like this:

Profit and Loss Account for G. Gladwin for the Year ended..(date)

Sales		62000
Opening stock of finished goods	17500	
Add production costs of finished goods	<u>39300</u>	
	56800	
Less closing stock of finished goods	<u>13750</u>	
		<u>43050</u>
Gross Profit		18950
<u>Less Expenses</u>		
Salaries of office staff	5000	
Commission for salesmen	6500	
Tax & insurance for van	<u>400</u>	
		<u>11900</u>
Net Profit		7050

Fig 21. From manufacturing to profit and loss account.

Now you try one:

B.Best's account

Construct the manufacturing and trading and profit and loss account from the following figures for B.Best:

Stock of raw materials at start	3000
Purchases of raw materials	9000
Stock of raw materials at end	4000
Carriage costs of bringing raw materials	500
Direct wages	7000
Indirect factory expenses	3000
Canteen expenses	1000
Sales	40000
Opening stock of finished goods	5000
Closing stock of finished goods	3500
Administration expenses	6000
Selling and distribution expenses	7500
Depreciation of office equipment	500
Provision for bad debts	350

9
Club Accounts

The title really should be 'The Accounts of Non–Profit making Organisations.' Rather a mouthful, but describes the main difference between these accounts and business accounts. The purpose of a club is for the enjoyment and benefit of its members, not to make a profit. Of course these accounts also apply to other non-profit making organisations .

RECEIPTS AND PAYMENTS ACCOUNT

Most club treasurers will keep lists of **receipts** and **payments**. This may be just the cash book. This will only record the actual amounts received and paid. You know, from your knowledge of profit and loss accounts, that when accounting for a period, you must include any amount relating to that period. This is regardless of whether it is paid or not. Therefore the receipts and payments account is not sufficient in itself. We have to prepare another account.

INCOME AND EXPENDITURE ACCOUNT

The trading and profit and loss account would be inappropriate, so we prepare an **income and expenditure account** instead. This is really just two lists:

- firstly the income,
- then the expenditure.

The result is called either the **surplus**Error! Bookmark not defined. or **deficit**. If income is greater its a surplus, if not, a deficit. If there are items on both lists which relate to each other, it is good practice to put them together in whichever list they will then apply to. For example, if there are receipts from dance tickets of £350 and dance expenses of £300, then these can be put together as a dance profit in the income list. Note that it is quite all right to refer to profit in these cases.

Note how the following receipts and payments account has been converted into an income and expenditure account:

Receipts and Payments Account   Fig 22

Receipts		Payments	
Cash at bank	250	Dance expenses	70
Cash in hand	30	Electricity	97
Subscriptions	60	Postages	7
Sale of dance tickets	110	Insurance	50
Fund raising event	72		

Income and Expenditure Account Fig 23

Income

Subscriptions		60
Sale of dance tickets	110	
Less dance expenses	<u>70</u>	
Profit on dance		40
Fund raising event		<u>72</u>
		172

Expenditure

Electricity		97
Postages		7
Insurance		<u>50</u>
		<u>154</u>
Surplus of income over expenditure		**18**

Note how the totals are written to the right, to enable deduction of the expenditure from the income.

Don't forget that you must always account for prepayments and accruals, just as in the profit and loss account.

It may sometimes be necessary to do a small trading account to ascertain how much of something was used during the period. eg Supposing a table tennis club had a stock of table tennis balls of 500 at the start of the year, bought 350 during the year and had 300 left at the end. This would mean that they had used 550 during the year. We would want to charge 550 in the expenditure account for that year, even though only 350 had been bought. ie stock at start, plus purchases less stock at end.

Try and construct an Income and Expenditure account from the figures of the Wolds Way Rambling Club:

Receipts and Payments Account

Subscriptions received	250	Fees for speaker	25
Income from coffee morning	65	Rent for village halls	35
Sale of rucksacks	350	Purchase of rucksacks	200
Takings from refreshments	15	Refreshments bought	7
Stock of tea, coffee etc. at end of year	12	Stock of refreshments at beginning of year	10

(answer in back of book)

Clubs also have balance sheets, just like any other organisation. You should have no problem with these by now. It is important to remember that anything paid in advance (by the club) is a current asset, and money still owing (by the club) is a current liability.

An Exercise

Below is an exam question from the London East Anglian Board, May 1989 paper 2, question 4.

On 1 January 1988 the Radcliffe Social Club had £890 in the bank. It had no other assets or liabilities. The following additional information is available during the year ended 31 December 1988

Subscription received (Of the above £150 is in advance for the next year.)	3200
Rates on club house paid	670
New furniture purchased (£2500 has been paid, the balance is on credit, repayable within one year.)	5000
Lighting and heating paid during the year	860

Receipts from admission to non–members for special shows	46000
Fees paid to performers at special shows	38500

On 31 December 1988 an electricity amount of £90 was unpaid.

a. Prepare for the year ended 31 December 1988:
   1. A receipts and payments account
   2. An income and expenditure account

b. Prepare a balance sheet as at 31 December 1988

10
Partnerships

Partnerships are formed for various reasons. The most obvious are :

1. A sharing of different areas of expertise. eg An upholsterer and a carpenter may start making furniture.

2. To share the work load, especially to gain holidays/weekends. Doctors often form partnerships.

3. To gain more capital – one person may not have enough on their own.

Capital

Each partner may put in a different amount of capital. It therefore seems fair to to award interest on capital. This is usually done at the rate they would have got if they had invested the money in ,say, a building society. A percentage rate is usually decided upon.

Salaries

These may or may not be paid to partners. If they are, this will probably be in proportion to the work done by them for the business.

Drawings

Just as a sole trader takes drawings, so may the partners. In a partnership it is usual to charge interest on these drawings. This is to discourage them from drawing too much money out of the business. As with interest on capital, a percentage rate is decided upon. It may be charged only for the months left in the financial year. Suppose the financial year is Jan to Dec, and a partner takes some drawings in August. He will be charged interest for five months – Aug to Dec.

Sleeping Partner

A sleeping partner is someone who invests money in the business, but also has limited liability. This means that if, say he had invested £10,000 and the business went bankrupt owing £400,000, he would only be liable for his £10,000 – this is the maximum he could lose. The others would have to pay the rest of the debt even if this meant losing their homes and possessions. The sleeping partner, however, cannot take part in the management of the business. He has no say at all about how it is run.

Deed of Partnership

You often think of a partnership as being two people, but, in fact, a business partnership may have between two and twenty people in it. When a partnership is formed, a document called a Deed of Partnership is drawn up. This details various agreements about holidays, interest allowed on capital, interest charged on drawings and the ratio in which the profit is shared.

Under the Partnership Act 1890 there are five rules which have to be followed in the event of there being **NO** Deed of Partnership. This rarely happens, as it is obviously desirable to have a deed drawn up. The five rules are :

1. No salaries allowed
2. No interest on drawings
3. No interest on capitals
4. If a partner puts in more than the agreed amount of capital then he will be paid 5% interest <u>on the extra amount only.</u>
5. Partners equally share profits and losses.

Appropriation Account

The difference between the accounts of partnerships and sole traders is in the way the profit is shared, or **appropriated**, after the net profit figure is ascertained. This is done by drawing up an **appropriation account**. When this is done by itself, beginning with the net profit figure, then the title is :

Appropriation Account for (Names) for the year ended (date).

If, however, you are drawing up the appropriation account along with the profit and loss account then the title is :

Profit and Loss Appropriation Account for (Names) for the year ended (date).

You do *not* put any titles in the middle of the accounts. Study the appropriation account drawn up from the following information.

The partnership of T.Dunne and B.Cowan.

Net profit	20,000
Salary for Cowan	5,000
Interest on drawings :	
Dunne	500
Cowan	350
Interest on capital:	
Dunne	600
Cowan	400

Profit to be shared in the ratio of Dunne three fifths, Cowan two fifths.

The example below shows how this is done.

Fig 24 shows how it should be done:

Appropriation account for Dunne and Cowan for the year ended (date)

Net profit		20000
Add interest charged on drawings:		
Dunne	500	
Cowan	<u>350</u>	
		<u>850</u>
		20850
Less salary for Cowan	5000	
Less interest paid on capitals:		
Dunne	600	
Cowan	<u>400</u>	
	1000	
		<u>6000</u>
		14850
Share of profits:		
Dunne 3/5 (14850 ÷ by 5 then x 3)	8910	
Cowan 2/5	<u>5940</u>	
		14850

SUMMARY

- Anything to add on must be accounted for first
- After everything else has been paid out, the remaining capital is shared in the agreed ratio.

Now you try this one:

Partnership Appropriation Account of Green, Cross and Bowles

Net Profit	35000
Interest on drawings:	
Green	600
Cross	400
Bowles	400
Salary for Green	12000
Interest on capital:	
Green	400
Cross	500
Bowles	500

Profit to be shared :
Cross & Bowles 40% each
Green 20%

CAPITAL ACCOUNTS AND CURRENT ACCOUNTS

When the owner of a business puts money into the business, a **capital account** is started. The capital account represents what the business owes to the owner. (This was explained in Chapter 2.)

All the amounts of interest on drawings, interest on capital and so on, must be entered on the capital account. In order to keep the capital accounts clear, a **current account** is opened for each partner. This must not be confused with the current account at the bank. The purpose of a partner's current account is to account for all the details which happen each year.

So each partner has a current account, as well as a capital account. The capital account remains fixed. It records the amount of capital which that partner put into the business, and remains the same. It is the current account which fluctuates with all the yearly happenings.

Suppose that Green, Cross and Bowles each had taken drawings of 6000, 4000 and 4000 respectively. Suppose also that their current accounts had credit balances of £2000, £1000 and £1000. If they had each put in capital of £40000, £50000 and £50000, their capital accounts would merely show this. Their capital and current accounts would look like this:

Fig 25. Capital and Current accounts

Capital Accounts:

Green	Dr	Cr	Bal
Bank		40000	40000cr

Cross	Dr	Cr	Bal
Bank		50000	5000cr

Bowles	Dr	Cr	Bal
Bank		50000	50000cr

OR

The capital accounts could be written like this:

Bowles

	Dr	Cr
Bank		5000
To C/d (balancing figure)	5000	
	5000	5000
Bal B/d		5000

Current Accounts:

Green

	Dr	Cr
Balance		2000
Drawings	6000	
Interest on drawings	600	
Salary		12000
Interest on capital		400
Share of profit		4600
Bal to c/d (balancing figure)	12400	
	19000	19000
Bal b/d		12400

Cross

Balance		1000
Drawings	4000	
Interest on drawings	400	
Salary		0
Interest on capital		500
Share of profit		9200
Bal to c/d	6300	
	10700	10700
Bal b/d		6300

Bowles

Balance		1000
Drawings	4000	
Interest on drawings	400	
Salary		0
Interest on capital		500
Share of profit		9200
Bal to c/d	6300	
	10700	10700
Bal b/d		6300

Note: As an alternative style you could write up the accounts in the three column running balance. Here is an example of one of them:-

Bowles   Dr   Cr   Bal

	Dr	Cr	Bal
Balance		1000	1000cr
Drawings	4000		3000
Interest on drawings	400		3400
Salary		0	3400
Interest on capital		500	2900
Share of profit		9200	6300cr

> Instead of carrying figures down you can simply put in a running total at the right. Some people find it useful to do this in pencil, or on their calculator, anyway, to check their c/d figures.

You will notice that, just as a capital account should have a credit balance, so should the current accounts. This represents what the business owes to the owner. If there is a debit balance, then the partner owes to the business.

An exercise to try:-

This is an old exam question from London East Anglian Group, May 1989.

Explain the meaning of:

- drawings
- interest on drawings
- provision for depreciation
- working capital
- interest on capital

Bunker and Lake are partners in a consultancy business. The following balances appear in their books at 31 December 1988 (after extraction of the trading and profit and loss accounts):

Capital accounts (1Jan 1988)	£
Bunker	40000
Lake	50000

Current accounts (1Jan1988)	
Bunker	8400cr
Lake	4120dr

Drawings (for the year ended 31 December 1988)	
Bunker	24000

Lake	30000
Motor van at cost	12000
Provision for depreciation on motor van	9000
Premises	100000
Cash at bank	6596
Wages accrued	3936
Debtors	6420
Bank loan (repayable in 1990)	30000
Interest owing on bank loan	1200
Net trading profit	40600
Interest on drawings:	
Bunker	400
Lake	1800

The partners had agreed to allow 8% per annum interest on capital and to share profits equally.

1) For the year ended 31 December 1988 prepare:
   a) The profit and loss appropriation of the partnership
   b) Each partner's current account

2) Prepare the balance sheet of the partnership as at 31st December 1988.

11
Appropriation Accounts of Plc and Ltd

The last chapter examined the accounts of partnerships. You know what a partnership is, and how it works.

- What does **Plc** mean ?
- What is **Ltd** ?

Ltd means limited. It is the liability of the owners which is limited. Who are the owners? The owners are the people who own **shares** in the business. Suppose a partnership has become very large with a lot of debts, and a lot of people owing money to it. If that partnership 'went bust' i.e. one of its creditors (usually a bank) calls for its money within a certain time and the business cannot pay it in that time, then the owners will be declared **bankrupt** . The business will be put into the hands of **receivers** who will sell off all the assets to pay the creditors as much of the money owed to them as possible. This may include the personal belongings of the owners, such as their houses and cars.

LIMITED COMPANIES
Of course, there is a way to lessen this catastrophe. The business can become a **limited company** This will mean that the owners' liability is limited to the amount of shares they own. If you owned £5000 worth of shares in your company, and it went bankrupt, you would only be expected to pay the £5000.

Private Limited Company

Ltd means **private limited company**. The issue of shares is to people whom you invite to buy them, not the general public. The shares of Private Limited Companies are often kept in the same family. If the business was previously a partnership, the partners will probably become the share holders. A share is literally a share in the business. This is also a useful way of raising extra capital.

How do you register a company?

Memorandum of Association

You have to send a **Memorandum of Association** to the **Registrar of Companies** in London. This must give:

- the name of the company,
- its address,
- the aims and objectives of the company,
- and the amount of money it would eventually like to raise through the sale of shares. This amount of money is called **authorised share capital.**

Articles of Association

You also have to send them your **Articles of Association** This will be the details of:

- share holders
- voting rights,
- the way the directors are appointed,
- and details about **dividends** Dividends are the share of profit given to share holders each year, usually calculated as a percentage.

If these documents are approved, the Registrar will issue a **certificate of incorporation**.

It is usual to ask a solicitor to draw up the documents for you, and this can be expensive. That is why some people buy **'off the peg ' companies** – already formed, with a name.

Public Limited Company

Plc means Public Limited Company. The shares are offered on the open market for anyone to buy. When someone has over 50 per cent of the shares, they are deemed to be in control of the company. Voting rights are linked to share ownership. When a Public Limited Company is registered, it will be issued with a **trading certificate** , as well as the certificate of incorporation.

SUMMARY OF LIMITED COMPANIES
- Private Limited Company means shares sold by invitation only.
- Public Limited Company means that shares are sold on the open market, so someone else could gain control, unless you keep more than 50 per cent yourself.
- Authorised share capital is the maximum amount which can be raised by issue of shares, as stated in the Memorandum of Association.
- Dividends are the share of profits given to shareholders each year.

WHAT SHOULD I KNOW ABOUT SHARES?

There are different types of shares. A shareholder of **ordinary shares** will do well in years where the company makes a large profit, but in bad years they may not receive any dividend at all. This is decided by the directors.

The **preference share** is a safer investment. As the name suggests, they take preference over ordinary shares. They are paid out first, then the remainder is shared out to the ordinary shareholders. However, the preference share always carries a fixed percentage, and they will be paid that percentage, even though the ordinary shareholders may be getting more.

Share premium

Shares are issued at a certain cost (the **nominal value**). Sometimes a company can make a 'profit' by selling shares at more than their nominal value. Suppose a company issued 100 ordinary shares for £1 each. It then finds that it can sell another 50 at £1.50 each. The extra £25 it will have raised is called **share premium**. This share premium is used to fund dividends in bad years, or sometimes to fund a bonus issue of shares.

Bonus Issue

A **bonus issue** is a free issue of shares to existing shareholders. This is usually based on the number of shares they hold. If you owned 100 shares, and the company was giving a bonus issue, they may give something like one free share for every ten held. You would then be given ten free shares.

Issued Share Capital

This is the amount of money which has actually been raised from the sale of shares.

Called Up Capital

Sometimes a company may sell its shares in instalments. These are known as 'calls.' A person may have decided to buy 100 £1 shares. He may pay the first 'call' of £50 in January, and contract to pay the other £50 in June. In between these dates you would say the the **called up capital** was £50.

DEBENTURES

Another way for companies to raise money(capital) is by issuing **debentures**. A debenture really is a sort of IOU:

- The company owes the debenture holder the amount of money on the debenture.
- The company will have to pay interest to the debenture holders for the amount of money they are lending to them. Debentures usually have a fixed term, and a fixed amount of interest. If you have a 10 year 6 per cent debenture, which cost you £100,, the company will have to pay you 6 per cent of that £100 for the next 10 years. It will then have to give you your £100 back.

RESERVES

Sometimes the directors of a company will decide to transfer some of the profit to a **reserve fund**. It is always wise to try to build up reserves, as these can be used to fund new projects and promote growth of the company.

HOW DO YOU TREAT SHARES IN THE ACCOUNTS?

As an example, suppose a company has an authorised share capital of £100,000 divided into 25,000 ten per cent preference shares of £1 each and 75,000 ordinary shares of £1 each.

All the preference shares are issued and fully paid, but only 50,000 of the ordinary shares are issued.

If the company made a good profit, paid the dividend on the preference shares and declared a dividend of nine per cent on the ordinary shares, how much money would be required for distribution?

There would be 25,000 preference shares X 10% = 2500
Add 50,000 X 9%   = 4500
Answer   7000

Now try this one

N.Rose & Co

Another company, N.Rose & Co., has an authorised share capital of £250,000 divided into 100,000 eight per cent preference shares and 150,000 ordinary shares.

The issued capital is 75,000 preference shares and 100,000 ordinary shares. It was decided to give twelve per cent dividend on the ordinary shares. How much would be required for distribution?

You must learn how this is shown in the accounts. Unlike the partnership accounts, the appropriation accounts of Plc and Ltd companies often leave an unappropriated amount on the Profit and Loss account to carry forward to the following year. This means that when you start the appropriation account with net profit, you must remember to add any unappropriated profit left from last year.

An example of shares in the accounts

Brown Ltd had a balance of unappropriated profit of £5000. This year the net profit was £2890. The authorised share capital was £10,000. Issued share capital was 3000 ten per cent preference shares(£1 each) and 5000 ordinary shares (£1 each). The directors decided to transfer £3000 to the general reserve. They recommended a dividend of eight per cent on the ordinary shares.

The appropriation account would look like this :

Unappropriated profit B/Fwd	5000
Net profit	2890
	7890
Transfer to general reserve	3000
	4890
Preference dividend(10%X3000)	300
	4590
Ordinary dividend (8%X5000)	400
Unappropriated profit	4190

When writing a balance sheet, the 'financed by' section will now have to contain the details of the share capital. The authorised share capital must always be shown, but not added in. Therefore you show the authorised share capital and then underline it to show that you are not including it in your calculations. The issued share capital will be shown and accounted for.

Note the example below:

Balance sheet as at..(date)

Fixed Assets			
Equipment			10000
Current Assets			
Stock	5870		
Debtors	10834		
Bank	5700		
Cash	206		
		22610	
Current Liabilities			
Creditors	12000		
Proposed Dividends	700		
		12700	
			9910
			19910
Financed By:			
Authorised share capital			10000
Issued share capital:			
Preference shares		3000	
Ordinary shares		5000	
			8000
General reserve		7720	
Unappropriated profit		4190	
			11910
			19910

Fig 26. Showing the treatment of shares on the balance sheet.

Now you try to answer the following question from an old exam paper:

From the information given below you are required to prepare for Streamline plc

    a. Profit and Loss Appropriation account for the year ended 31 December 1990;
    b. Balance Sheet as at 31 December 1990.

Streamline plc has an authorised share capital of £520 000, divided into 500 000 £1 ordinary shares and 20 000 5% preference shares of £1 each. Of these shares, 300 000 ordinary shares and all of the 5% preference shares have been issued and are fully paid.

In addition to the above information, the following balances remained in the accounts after the Profit and Loss account had been prepared for the year ended 31 December 1990.

	Dr £	Cr £
Plant and machinery at cost	140 000	
Provision for depreciation on plant and machinery		50 000
Premises at cost	250 000	
Profit and Loss account balance (1 January 1990)		34 000
Net trading profit for year ended 31 December 1990		15 000
Wages owing		3 900
Bank balance	15 280	
Stock (31 December 1990)	16 540	
Trade debtors and creditors	12 080	3 000
Advertising prepaid	2 000	
General reserve		10 000

The directors have proposed the payment of the preference share dividend, and an ordinary share dividend of 6%. They also recommend a transfer of £20 000 to the general reserve.

12
Interpretation Of Final Accounts

The whole purpose of final accounts is to assess how well the business is performing. The profit and loss account tells you how much profit you have made. The balance sheet tells you how the business stands at a particular date. However, before you begin to look at the final accounts, it would be as well to remind ourselves of their limitations.

WORKING OUT PROFIT

The profit shown by the profit and loss account bears no relation to the amount of money you actually have in the bank. This is because of the following :

- Stock. The stock figures used are based upon the firm's method of valuation of its stock. (See note at end of chapter) They also depend on the accuracy of the stocktaking.
- Depreciation. Depreciation is based upon estimated values.
- Doubtful debts. The provision for doubtful debts is only an estimated figure.

These three points are variable; a different accountant may arrive at a different profit figure. This seems a difficult concept to grasp. Most people believe that only one answer could be correct, but this is not so.

Fixed Assets
The cost of the asset is a known and definite figure, but the depreciation is an estimated figure. Therefore the net figure used is an estimated figure.

Current Assets
Stock could vary as stated under profit.

Debtors figure takes into account doubtful debts which are an estimated figure.

Interpreting the final accounts

In spite of all these variables, you <u>can</u> interpret the final accounts and obtain a fair view of the state of the business. Suppose you were considering investing in a company. Consider the balance sheet like this:

Fixed Assets

- Is the depreciation realistic?
- Are new assets being purchased? Are old ones being written off? (or depreciated to nothing)
- Are there plenty of worthwhile assets? – do they own the premises?

Current Assets

- Is there a sensible balance between stock, debtors, bank and cash? i.e. beware too high a debtors figure (except in the case of a firm making Easter eggs which may have a high debtors figure and low stock just after Easter!)
- Is the stock figure too high – too much money tied up in it? Or too low – orders could be lost through delay. Could be low due to lack of funds.
- Is the debtors figure increasing – if so, is there a corresponding increase in sales? Are bad debts increasing? Should better discounts be offered to encourage prompt payment?
- Bank/cash – Is there a large balance? If so should this be employed elsewhere? On the other hand, shortages mean that you can't buy in great bulk and obtain good discounts etc.
- Creditors – Are they increasing? Is this because of shortage of funds? It could be due to heavy buying just before a peak period e.g. Christmas, or that the firm is trying to expand. You would want to find out if they had been outstanding for very long, and if they were pressing for payment.
- Are reserves being built up? Is profit being put back into the business? How much does the company owe in long term loans ?

USING RATIOS

To analyse even further, these ratios can be used:–

To test for efficiency

Return on capital employed = $\dfrac{\text{Profit} \times 100}{\text{Capital employed}}$

Note –Capital employed is the Capital figure used in the balance sheet i.e. Owner's capital, partners' capital accounts or issued share capital, depending on the type of business. (This figure should not include long term loans).

Gross profit ratio = $\dfrac{\text{Gross Profit} \times 100}{\text{Sales}}$

Net Profit ratio = $\dfrac{\text{Net Profit} \times 100}{\text{Sales}}$

Working capital = Current assets less current liabilities

To test for solvency

Current ratio = $\dfrac{\text{Current assets}}{\text{Current liabilities}}$

(Ideal is said to be 2:1 – that is CA: CL)

Acid test (or quick asset) ratio = $\dfrac{\text{Current assets less stock}}{\text{Current liabilities}}$

Rate of stock turnover = $\dfrac{\text{Cost of sales}}{\text{Average stock}}$

To calculate capital

Owners capital/shareholders funds =
- Capital at start + net profit less drawings;
- OR Capital accounts + current accounts;
- OR Issued shares + reserves;

Which one of those three methods is used, of course, depends on the type of business: sole trader, partnership or limited company.

An Exercise to try

The following is taken from the NEA 1988 exam paper. Try it and then check your answers with those at the back of the book.

On 31 May 1988 Fiona Maxwell presents you with copies of balance sheets of two engineering firms. She says that she is thinking of expanding her light engineering business by taking over one of these firms and she asks you for advice. The balance sheets are shown below.

Metal Products Ltd

Balance Sheet as at 30 September 1987

	£
Premises at cost	15000
Machinery at cost	5000
Stock at cost (market value £3000)	2000
Debtors	1800
Bank balance	200
	24000
Share capital: Authorised and issued	19360
Undistributed profits	2640
Creditors	2000
	24000

Forge Engineering Ltd
Balance Sheet as at 30 June 1987

Premises at cost		35000
Machinery at cost less depreciation		15000
Stock at cost (market value £12000)	20000	
Debtors	9000	
Less provision for doubtful debts	1000	
	8000	
		28000
		78000
Share capital: Authorised and issued		63800
Undistributed profits		4200
Creditors		8000
Bank Overdraft		2000
		78000

Prepare a report which should include the following points.

   a) A criticism of the information shown in the balance sheets.

   b) An explanation of additional accounting information which is required.

   c) Any calculations you think would be useful.

   d) A recommendation as to whether either firm should be taken over, giving your reasons.

Note that criticism in this question does not mean a criticism of the layout, but rather an appraisal of the contents.

STOCK VALUATION

As mentioned earlier in the book, stock is always valued at cost price (or selling price if it is lower). However, it is not always so easy to work this out. Suppose you have a box full of brass screws. You have bought some at four pence each. A month later, you buy some more at six pence each. You keep them all in the same box. It is not always easy to know which cost four pence and which cost six pence. You will not wish to label every screw!

There are three ways of costing your screws:

- FIFO , first in, fist out;

- LIFO , last in first out and

- AVCO average cost.

With FIFO you would assume that the first screws you take out cost four pence (you will know how many of each you should have.)

With LIFO you will assume that the first ones you take out cost six pence.

With AVCO you would assume that all the screws cost five pence (4+6 divided by 2).

Obviously, the value of your stock would depend on which of these methods you are using. You must use the same method each year – consistency concept.

13
Funds Flow Statements

There is another method of interpretation of final accounts, which is effective if you have access to two years accounts for comparison. It is called a Funds Flow Statement, and consists of two lists –

- sources of funds
- application of funds.

These are compiled from the increases or decreases of the various components of the balance sheet.

SOURCES OF FUNDS

A fairly obvious source of funds is an increase in a loan.
Another obvious source is the net profit for the year.

Much less obvious is that an increase in creditors is a source of funds. This is because you have gained something from the creditors without (yet) paying for it.

APPLICATION OF FUNDS

An increase in fixed assets would be an application of funds, as this must mean that new assets have been purchased.
An increase in stock would be an application of funds, as you must have spent some money on more stock.

An increase in debtors is less obvious. You have had the expense of outlay without yet receiving any recompense so this is an application of funds. Drawings are an application of course.

WORKING IT OUT

It is all very logical, but needs some thought. Some people understand this immediately, while others always have to argue with themselves. Don't worry if you are one of the latter. You are certainly not alone.

Look at the two balance sheets of G.Bunter in Fig 27

Now you can do your flow of funds statement. Sometimes this is called a **sources and applications of funds statement**.

See Fig 28 on next page.

Note that the statement is labelled as at the date of the second year. Obviously you could not do this after the first year ! This is why the profit figure used is that of the second year. Also the drawings figure is that of the second year.

Fig. 27 Balance sheets of G Bunter.

	Year 1			Year 2		
Fixed Assets			5000			6120
Current Assets						
Stock	3750			4250		
Debtors	2890			3450		
Bank	280			2040		
		6920			9740	
Current Liabilities						
Creditors		2725			2950	
			4195			6790
			9195			12910
Financed by:						
Capital at start	6745			9195		
Less drawings	1000			2000		
		5745			7195	
Add net profit		3450			5715	
			9195			12910

109

Fig 28. Flow of Funds Statement for G Bunter as at (date of year 2)

Sources of funds		
Net profit		5715
Increase in creditors		225
		5940
Application of Funds		
Increase in fixed assets	1120	
Increase in debtors	560	
Increase in stock	500	
Drawings	2000	
	4180	
Excess of sources over application		1760
Proof		
Bank at start	280	
Bank at end	2040	
Increase in bank	(1760)	

SUMMARY

- Increase in fixed assets must mean that money has been spent buying new assets. Therefore this is an application of funds.

- The same applies to increase in stock.

- The increase in debtors is an application of funds because you have had to spend in order to supply, and have not yet been paid.

- The drawings are an obvious application.

- Decrease in creditors means you have spent money to pay some of them off, so it is an application.

- Note that the difference in cash and bank in year 1 and year 2 proves that your statement is correct.

Examples to try

Now try some yourself. You will find the answers in the back of the book.

Fig 29 Practice sheet for flow of funds statement (1)

Balance sheet of KS alarms

	Year 1			Year 2	
Fixed Assets		30000			50000
Current Assets					
Stock	7000			12000	
Debtors	3500			6000	
Bank	12000			5000	
		22500			23000
Current Liabilities					
Creditors	3700			10500	
			18800		12500
			48800		62500
Financed by:					
Capital at start		40000			48800
Add net profit		8800			9700
Loan		0			4000
			48800		62500

Fig 30. Practice sheet for flow of funds statement (2)

Balance sheet of J Bird

	Year 1			Year 2		
Fixed Assets			35000			45000
Current Assets						
Stock	3700			5350		
Debtors	5200			7500		
Bank	2000			0.00		
		10900			12850	
Current Liabilities						
Creditors	2500			3200		
Bank o/d	0			1500		
					4700	
			8400			8150
			43400			53150
Financed by:						
Capital at start			45000			43400
Add net profit			10500			14500
			55500			57900
Less drawings			12100			4750
			43400			53150

14
Incomplete Records

Many businesses do not keep complete accounting records. They may have a cash book. Quite commonly an analysed cash book is used. In this, there are many columns across the page pertaining to the different expenses of the business.

If all sales are cash sales, and double entry book-keeping is not necessary and therefore an analysed cash book is a pretty good way to go about things. The totals at the foot of the page will be equivalent to the various accounts.

Some small firms just put all paperwork on one side in a file. Sometimes everything is impaled on a spike in a block of wood for safe keeping until someone has time to do something about it.

It is very costly to ask an accountant to come and sort that lot out. A freelance book keeper can find him/herself very much in demand. Therefore you should find this chapter especially useful in your future work, as well as for any exams you may take.

You must collect as much information you as you can. Till receipts, cheque book stubs, general receipts and so on. Now, from this heap of assorted 'evidence' you must try to write up some correct accounts.

Darren Thompson has been trading for a year now. He sells computer software from a small shop which has been lent to him rent free for two years. When he started he had saved up £1500 and was given another £500 to help him get started. He bought some shelving for £500. His starting stock of software cost him £2000 and he was able to buy this on credit from Skyway Products. He bought a second hand till for £350.

Now, after one year's trading you can gather the following information:

- Money taken over the counter had amounted to £10000.
- He had paid his creditors (Skyway Products) a total of £5000
- Running expenses such as electricity and telephone came to £649
- Money owing to Skyway was £1560
- Darren had taken out £1500 in drawings
- His stock was now worth £1975

STATEMENT OF AFFAIRS

The first thing you must do is to prepare a Statement of Affairs as at the starting date. This is a very basic sort of Balance Sheet. Darren's would look like this :

Till	350
Stock	2000
Shelves	500
Cash (after buying above)	1150
	4000
Creditor	
Skyway Products	2000
Net worth (Capital)	2000

You need to find the figures for sales and purchases so that you can prepare the Trading and Profit and Loss Accounts.

To find the sales figure

To find the sales figure in Darren's case is easy: it is his takings of £10000.
If he had been selling things on credit , you would have:

- taken the figure received from debtors,
- deducted debtors at start of year,
- added debtors at end of year.

This would have given you the true figure for *this* year. Debtors at start would belong to last years account, debtors at end to this year.

To find the purchases figure

Use the same principle.
The cash paid to creditors was   5000

Less owing at start	2000
	3000
Add owing at end	1560
Purchases for year	= 4560

Now you have what you need to construct the Trading and Profit and Loss Account.

Sales		10000
Stock at start	2000	
Add purchases	4560	
	6560	
Less closing stock	1975	
		4585
Gross profit		5415
Expenses		649
Net profit		4766

Before you can do the Balance Sheet, you will have to check that the cash he has (either in hand or at the bank) is exactly the amount it should be.

Just do a simple cash book as in Figure 31, on next page.

Fig.31. Cash Book.

Balance at start	1150	Cash paid to creditor	5000
Received from cash sales	10000	Expenses	649
		Drawings	1500
	1500		
		Balance to c/d	4001
	11150		11150

Balance b/d   4001

Now the Balance Sheet can be set out.

Balance Sheet for Darren Thompson as at ...(date)
Fixed Assets
Till   350
Shelves   500
                                                    ———
                                                    850

Current Assets
Stock   1975
Cash   4001
                   ———
                                   5976
Current Liabilities
Creditor   1560
                                   ———
                                                   4416
                                                   ———
                                                   5266

Financed By :

Capital at start   2000
Add Net Profit   4766
                   ———
                   6766
Less drawings   1500
                   ———
                                                   5266

SUMMARY

- First gather as much information as possible.

- Next, get your starting point – do the Statement of Affairs.

- Now, begin to work through the final accounts for the year, working out some of the figures as you go.

It is not so difficult to achieve a full set of accounts providing that you have all the necessary basic information. There are times, of course, when you really have to estimate. A trader may not have a till which gives a print out. He may have taken drawings and not recorded it. He may have paid expenses out of the till, or taken goods from stock for his own use. This taking of stock is classed as drawings. It should be deducted from purchases in the Trading Account, as it reduces the amount of purchases used for the business.

Of course, if you are trying to sort out the bookkeeping as well as the final accounts, you will have a tougher job. Persistence is the key. You will have to find out who owes the business money. The creditors will soon contact you! With any luck, your businessman will have kept some record of money owing to him– even if it seems rather primitive to you. Just methodically sort through the 'evidence' putting it in date order first. Then you will have to ascertain who has paid their bills.

Unfortunately, sometimes people will pay their bills in the pub over a pint of beer or two. This way, your businessman will probably have used the proceeds. This is where tact and diplomacy are useful assets. Of necessity, you will soon acquire the necessary skills to winkle out unpaid bills, and not harass those who have paid.

Alfred Smith's Business

As always, the only way to check that you have really understood these methods, is to actually work one out.

The following information has been gathered about the business of Alfred Smith for the month of March:

Cash received from customers	53
Invoices sent for work completed:	
Mrs Jones	254
Mrs Ginn	110
Mr Glew	235
Mr Thompson	145
Expenses paid out:	
Materials	352
Overheads	178
Cash in Bank on March 31	976
Stock of unused materials at end of month	350
Stock of materials at start of month	490

Prepare a Trading and Profit and Loss Account and a Balance Sheet for Alfred for the month.

15
Mark Up And Margin

You will need to understand the relationship between **mark up** and **margin**. It is really quite simple. If you were to buy an article for say £8 and then sell it again for £12, the mark up and margin are both four pounds. However, the mark up is one half of the cost price but the margin, still four pounds, is a third of the selling price.

HOW DOES THIS APPLY TO ACCOUNTS ?

Look at this Trading Account :

Sales		3600
Stock at start	1000	
Purchases	2800	
	3800	
Stock at end	1400	
Cost of sales		2400
Gross Profit		1200

- What is the margin?
- What is the mark up?

The Margin is one third or 33⅓ per cent.

$$\frac{\text{Gross profit}}{\text{Sales}} = \frac{1200}{3600}$$

Similarly the Mark Up is one half or 50 per cent

$$\text{Mark Up} = \frac{\text{Gross profit}}{\text{Cost of sales}} = \frac{1200}{2400}$$

Fig.32. Mark up and margin.

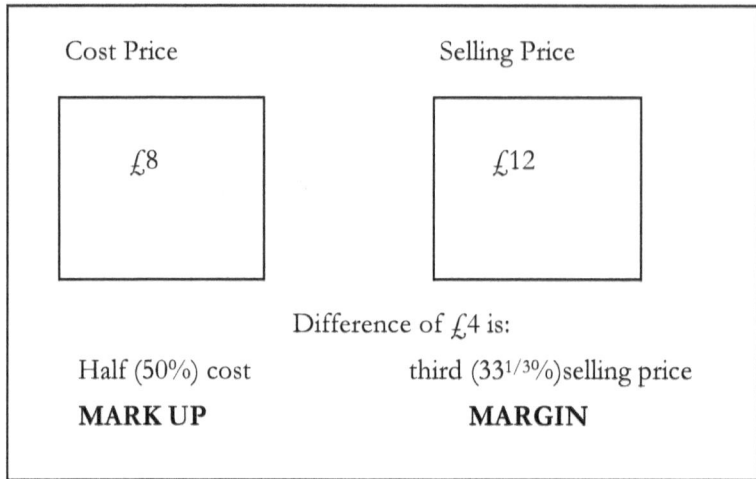

Here is another Trading Account:

Sales		22000
Opening Stock	1700	
Purchases	17000	
	18700	
Closing stock	2200	
		16500
Gross profit		5500

- What is the mark up and margin?
- What is the average stock?
- What is the turnover?

The Mark Up is one third.

The Margin is one quarter.

Note

These combinations always go together.

Mark up 1/3 Margin 1/4

Mark up 1/2 Margin 1/3

Mark up 1/4 Margin 1/5

Average stock is the two stock figures added together, then divided by two.

Turnover is just another word for Sales.

So the average stock is 1950 and the turnover is 22000.

SUMMARY

- The combinations of Mark Up and Margin always follow the same pattern, as described above.
- Mark Up is calculated on cost price; Margin on selling price.

Try the following:

Will Grant's account

Will Grant's Mark Up is 50 %

Average stock	3400
Purchases	2600
Opening stock	3200

Find out:
1. Closing stock
2. Gross profit
3. Sales.

Hint: Draw up a skeleton trading account and work backwards, filling in the blanks. The questions are in the order you'll need to progress.

Answer at the back of the book, but try to do it first !

An exam question from the NEA 1989 paper

Owing to pressure of work, Mr Singh postponed his stocktaking to Sunday 4 June 1989 although his financial year ended on 31 May 1989.

At 4 June he valued his stock at £7600 (cost price).

In the period 1 – 4 June:–
Purchases were £840

Takings at tills £820

Customer returned goods originally sold to him for £60

Goods sold on credit amounted to £280

Mr Singh took goods £30 cost price for own use

His gross profit is 25% of cost

Calculate the amount of stock at 31 May which should be shown in his trading account to 31 May 1989. Show all workings.

16
Bank Reconciliation

You now need to refer back to the cash book. This will be useful revision at this stage.

In addition to our cash book, you will have a further check on your cash position via statements from the bank. The statement from the bank will have the income and outgoings the opposite way round from your cash book.

Very likely, the balance on the statement will differ from that in the cash book. This is due to:

- **Unpresented cheques**: Cheques paid to people which do not yet appear on the bank statement.
- **Charges** made by the bank (unknown to us until now therefore not entered in cash book)
- **Dishonoured cheques**. Sometimes you will have received a cheque, paid it into the bank and had it returned marked 'Refer to drawer'(The drawer is the person who is paying.) This means that either there are insufficient funds in their account to cover the cheque, or there is a fault in the way the cheque was made out. The date could be in the future (post dated) or out of date (more than six months usually). The signature could be missing or incorrect or perhaps the amount in words does not tally with the amount in figures.

You therefore have to reconcile the cash book to the bank statement to check that our figures are correct and to obtain our true cash position.

DIFFERENT METHODS YOU CAN USE

There are three ways to do this process:

- Reconcile the cash book total to the bank statement.
- Reconcile the bank statement to the cash book.
- Obtain a corrected total for both which agrees.

The third method is the most common. First you work out the corrected cash book total. Then you also work out a corrected total for the bank statement. In other words, you begin with the cash book total, put on to it all the things on the bank statement that it does not contain. Then you start again with the bank statement total and put on it all the things in the cash book that are not on it.

An example:

Fig 33. Reconciling the cash book to the bank statement

The cash book:

Bal b/d	100.00		
S.Smith	50.00	B.Bates	200.00
P.Davies	20.00	R.Batty	59.00
R.Sinclair	152.00	G.Cresswell	19.00
B.Petty	47.00	M.D.T.Services	25.00
Cash paid into bank	50.00		
J.Johnson	56.00		
		Bal to c/d	172.00
	475.00		475.00
Bal b/d	172.00		

Bank Statement

Balance			100.00cr
Cash		50.00	150.00
cheque		50.00	200.00
cheque		20.00	220.00
cheque	200.00		20.00
cheque dishnd	152.00	152.00	20.00
cheque		47.00	67.00
charges	10.00		57.00cr

An example

This is the reconciliation of the totals in Fig.33

Using method 3: correct both cash book and bank statement
Step 1
You begin with the total of the bank column in the cash book.

		172.00
Less: Bank charges	10.00	
Less: Dishonoured cheque	152.00	
		162.00
Corrected balance		10.00

Step 2

Balance as per Bank Statement :–

		£57.00
Add cheque from J.Johnson		56.00
		113.00
Less cheques paid out	59.00	
(Not yet recorded by bank)	19.00	
	25.00	
		103.00
Corrected balance		10.00

Method 2: Reconcile the bank statement to the cash book

Balance as per bank statement		57.00
Add back charges		10.00
Add back dishonoured cheque		152.00
Add cheque rec'd not yet on statement		<u>56.00</u>
		275.00
Less unpresented cheques		
	59.00	
	19.00	
	<u>25.00</u>	
		<u>103.00</u>
Balance as cash book		172.00

To do **method 1**, simply begin with the cash book total and reverse the additions and subtractions above until you arrive at the bank statement total.

In each case you have taken the current balance and added or deducted items which have not yet been processed through our system. You have now arrived at the same balance for both.

On the cash book you had to deduct bank charges. These have not yet appeared in our cash book because they have not yet been entered from the bank statement. They will subsequently be entered in the credit (out) side of the cash book. You also deducted the dishonoured cheque. You had previously entered it in our cash book on the debit (in) side. Now that you won't be getting the money after all, you will eventually have to enter it into our cash book on the credit side to take it out again. In the meantime, you are only doing the reconciliation, so you deduct it from our cash book total.

Method 3 will give you the actual amount of cash in the bank.

Try the following:
Do a reconciliation based on the cash book and bank statement in Fig.34. on next page.

Fig 34

Details	Bank	Details	Bank
Bal b/d	138.00		
S.Naismith	100.00	L.Francis	98.00
P.Smith	9.00	F.Briggs	92.00
K.Petty	106.00	D.Brown	20.00
C.Ashton	92.00	J.Thompso	32.00
Cash paid into bank	50.00		
G.Robin	62.00		
		Bal to c/d	315.00
	557.00		557.00
Bal b/d	315.00		

Bank Statement

			138.00
Balance			
cheque (paid in)		100.00	
cheque		9.00	247.00
cheque (paid out)	98.00		149.00
cheque	92.00		57.00
cash		50.00	107.00
Standing order		37.00	144.00
cheque	20.00		124.00
charges	10.00		114.00

You could further practise by keeping a simple cash book of your personal expenses, then reconcile this with your bank statement.

Now try the following, which is an old exam question. (Northern Ireland Schools Examination Council 1988)

At the end of each month why will the cash book 'bank' balance differ from that appearing in the bank statement covering the same period? Give *four* reasons.

2. This is the bank account for the month of April of Jane who runs a small business.

Dr.				Jane's Bank Account			Cr.
Apr	3	Balance b/f	642·87	Apr	8	R. M. Jones	56·31
	3	Sales	267·31		8	Smith Stores Ltd	12·67
	28	Sales	189·43		8	M. Maguire	315·74
	31	Sales	210·50		8	L. Kelly	123·54
					15	M. R. Morgan	117·84
					15	Johnston & Black Ltd	159·74
					31	Balance	524·27
			£1310·11				£1310·11
May	1	Balance b/f	524·27				

Below is Jane's Bank Statement for April

JANE JOHNSTON
67 MARKET STREET
CASTLETOWN

IN ACCOUNT WITH
PROVINCE-WIDE BANK
WEST STREET
CASTLETOWN

Account No. 025 673 216

DATE	PARTICULARS	DEBIT	CREDIT	BALANCE
1988				
1	Balance forward			642·87
3	LTG		267·31	910·18
8	824	56·31		853·87
11	827	123·54		730·33
17	CT		26·89	757·22
19	826	315·74		441·48
20	828	117·84		323·64
21	SO	93·56		230·08
26	829	159·74		70·34
28	LTG		189·43	259·77
31	CG	18·50		241·27

DD Direct Debit   CT Credit Transfer   DR Overdrawn Balance
CD Cash Dispenser   CG Charges   SO Standing Order

Study both records of Jane's bank account and answer the questions which follow.

(i) Give Jane *three* reasons why her Bank Statement balance and the balance from her own bank account are not the same.

(a) ....

(b) ....

(c) .... (6)

(ii) Explain to Jane why the cheque numbers do not appear in the Bank Statement in the same order as they appear in her own record.

....

.... (4)

(iii) Use Jane's Bank Account on the opposite page to make any necessary entries to bring it up to date. (6)

(iv) In the space below prepare a Bank Reconciliation Statement. (10)

Fig. 35. Reconciliation exam question.

17
Working With Petty Cash

It is often necessary to deal with very small amounts of money. This includes cash to buy tea or coffee for use at work, bus fares and other expenses which should be charged to the business. The cash book could quickly become very complicated with all these minor amounts entered in it. Therefore the answer is to have a separate cash book for the minor transactions. This is known as a **petty cash book**.

IMPREST

Most firms operate their Petty Cash using what is known as the Imprest system (even if they don't call it that!). Imprest simply means float. Periodically, perhaps weekly or monthly, the person in charge of Petty Cash will be given a float. This is an amount of money.

PETTY CASH VOUCHERS

The Petty Cashier will also be given a pad of **petty cash vouchers.** Whenever the cashier issues anyone with some petty cash, a voucher is completed, signed by the recipient, and kept in the petty cash box. This means that at any time, the totals of the actual cash plus the amounts on the vouchers should equal the amount of the original float.

For example, suppose that you are in charge of the petty cash. You are given £50 float on the first of the month. During the month, someone asks you for £5 to buy some coffee and sugar. You write the details on the voucher, and the person signs it. (See Fig.36)

You will give the person the £5 and put the voucher in the cash box. Note that in the space marked Folio, you will begin your own numbering system.

If you now add up the cash you have left, you should have £45 plus a voucher for £5, which agrees with the original float of £50. You can see that throughout

129

the week/month there will be many transactions, and this system is a useful check on the cash.

Fig 36. Petty cash voucher

Petty Cash				
Signature B.Jones	Passed By GMH	Folio Number 1		
Date	Description	Job No.	Amount	
01/10	Cash to buy coffee and sugar	-	5	00
			5	00

THE PETTY CASH BOOK

Of course, these transactions are also recorded elsewhere. A special cash book is kept, called the Petty Cash Book. Fig. 37. shows an example.

The float is entered on the left, and all the transactions are analysed into the columns on the right. Your folio numbers are used here to identify the vouchers.

Fig.37. Example of a petty cash book

Float Rec'd	Date	Details	Voucher No.	Total	Postage	Office sundries	Cleaning	Stationery	Travel Exp.

Float Received	Date	details	voucher No.	total	postages	office sundries	cleaning	stationery	travelling expenses
	March								
50.00	1	Bank							
	2	Coffee and sugar	1	5.00		5.00			
	4	wnd.clnr	2	6.50			6.50		
	7	bus.fares	3	2.00					2.00
	10	stamps	4	11.00	11.00				
	15	clean.mtrls	5	6.00			6.00		
	20	petrol	6	10.00					10.00
	25	Milk pwdr	7	2.00		2.00			
	30	wnd.clnr	8	6.50			6.50		
				49.00	11.00	7.00	19.00		12.00
		to c/d		1.00					
50.00				50.00					
1.00	b/d								
49.00	bank								

Fig.38. Wold Green Florists petty cash book As an example, we will enter up the petty cash book of Wold Green Florists. During the month of March, their Petty Cash transactions were as follows :

1st March   Received imprest (float) of £50

2nd March   Paid out £5 for coffee and sugar

4th   March Paid window cleaner £6.50

7th   March Paid out bus fares of £2

10th March Bought stamps £11

15th March Paid out £6 for cleaning materials

20th March Paid out £10 petrol money for firm's mini bus

25th March Paid out £2 for milk powder

30th March Paid window cleaner £6.50 (again)

The Petty Cash Book will appear as in Figure 38.

Now the Petty Cashier will be given sufficient money to restore the float(imprest).

Now continue it yourselves:

April 1 Received money to restore the imprest

April 4 Paid out £4.50 for coffee

April 7 Paid window cleaner £6.50

April 10 Bought stamps £11

April 15 Bought a new pad of Petty Cash Vouchers £0.50

April 20 Paid out bus fares £2.75

April 24 Paid out £5 for biscuits for seminar

April 30 Paid window cleaner £6.50

How much imprest will you need ?

On the next two pages, you will find another question and the suggested layout for the petty cash book pages.

12. Brian Jones is in charge of the Petty Cash in his firm. The Petty Cash is run on the Imprest System with the amount being made up on the Friday afternoon each week. At the start of each week he has £25 in his cash box.

   (a) What proof does the firm have that Brian actually pays out the amounts entered in the Petty Cash Book and is not just putting the money in his own pocket?

   ....
   ....

   (b) Write up the Petty Cash Book for the week beginning 8 September from the details given above and the vouchers below.

   (c) Make the necessary entries to show how the Petty Cash Book is completed and balanced on the Friday afternoon. (31)

PETTY CASH		
Voucher No. 85	Date 8 Sept	
	£	p
Bus Fares City Centre	-	60
Total	-	60
Received by J Smith		

PETTY CASH		
Voucher No. 88	Date 10 Sept	
	£	p
Taxi to station Sale Manager	3	-
Total	3	-
Received by RL		

PETTY CASH		
Voucher No. 86	Date 5 Sept	
	£	p
2nd class stamps	1	30
Parcel	2	10
Total	3	40
Received by T Orr		

PETTY CASH		
Voucher No. 89	Date 10 Sept	
	£	p
Rail Fare Coleraine	10	-
Total	10	-
Received by JMB		

PETTY CASH		
Voucher No. 87	Date 9 Sept	
	£	p
Window cleaner	4	-
Total	4	-
Received by Pat Harrison		

PETTY CASH		
Voucher No. 90	Date 12 Sept	
	£	p
Stamps	2	10
Total	2	10
Received by T Orr		

Fig. 39. Petty cash exam question.

Receipts	Date	Details	Voucher Number	Total Payments	Cleaning	Postage	Travelling Expenses

PETTY CASH BOOK

Receipts	Date	Details	Voucher Number	Total Payments	Cleaning	Postage	Travelling Expenses

PETTY CASH BOOK

SUMMARY

- The Petty Cash system is designed to take care of the many small cash transactions of a business.
- The Imprest is the float, or amount of money given to the petty cashier periodically.
- The totals on the Petty Cash Vouchers plus the cash in the box should always equal the amount of the original float.
- All Petty Cash transactions are recorded in the Petty Cash Book.

18
Break Even Analysis

Break Even Point

As its name suggests, Break Even Analysis simply involves finding the point at which the business will break even. This means finding out what volume of sales is needed for the business to neither profit nor loss. The way to calculate this is to find out the total fixed costs, the variable costs per unit(item)sold and the number of items sold.

As an example, let's suppose that Shirley Minton makes teddy bears. Her fixed costs are £10000. Her selling price is £8 per teddy bear. The variable costs per teddy bear are £3 each. This variation could be due to such things as staff on piece work or fluctuating costs of materials. She expects to sell 10000 teddy bears. Shirley's break even point would be:

$$\frac{\text{Total fixed costs}}{\text{Selling price} - \text{variable cost}} = \frac{10000}{8 - 3}$$

The answer is 2000 units (teddy bears)

This means that Shirley must sell 2000 teddy bears just to break even. To make a profit she must make more.

This can be illustrated in a graph. See Fig.40 below.

Fig 40

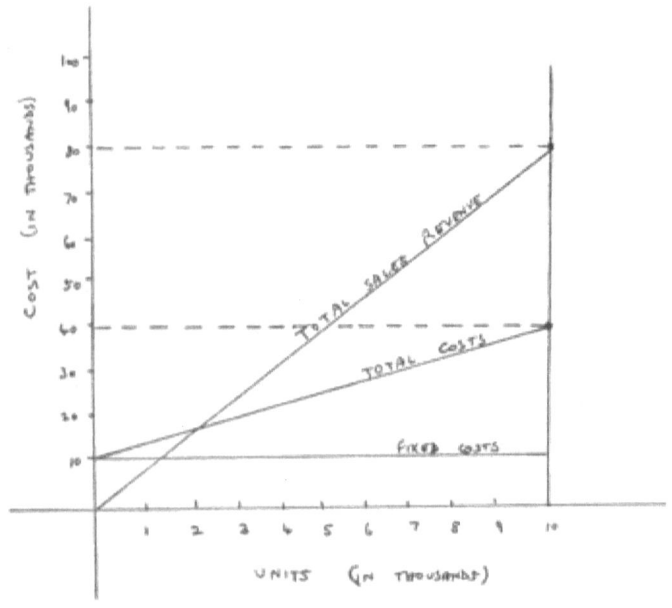

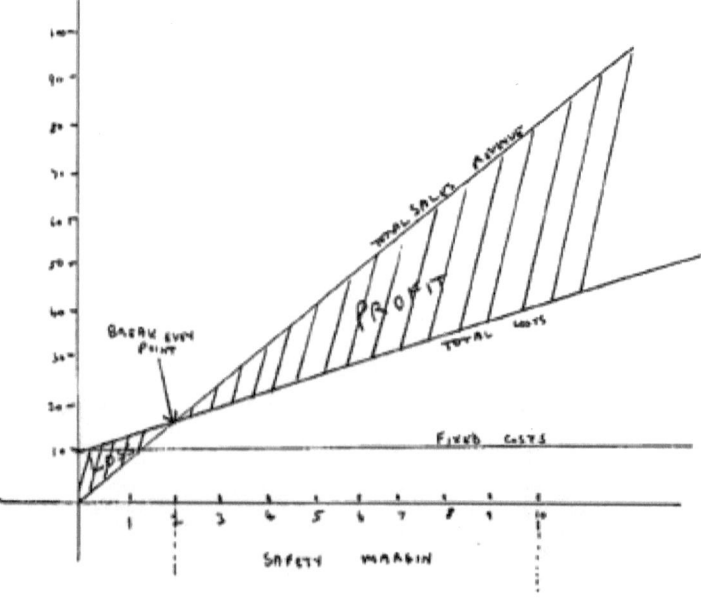

To plot sales revenue:
Expected sales x selling price = 80,000

plot from 10,000(expected sales) to 80,000

Draw a line from 0 to this point.

To plot total costs:
Variable costs x expected sales + fixed costs

= 10,000 x 3 + 10,000 = 40,000.

Plot from 10,000(expected sales) to 40,000

Draw a line from fixed costs(10,000) to this point.

The point where the two lines cross is break even point.

The graph is a very useful visual indication of a business's progress. Notice the names of the different lines and parts of the graph.

Now you try this one (do formula and graph):
Jason Rose produced this information about his business :

Total fixed costs £12000

Selling price per unit £10

Variable costs per unit £4

Expected sales 8000

Now try the following exam question from the Northern Ireland Schools Examination Council paper 3 1989 (question 3)

parts a–d.

3. Arnold has begun manufacturing computer desks and has presented you with the following information regarding his business for the year:

Direct Labour costs	£4 per desk
Raw Material costs	£12 per desk
Fixed Expenses	£1,000 per year
Selling price	£20 per desk

Anticipated units produced and sold during the year: 500.

REQUIRED

(a) Draw a 'break-even graph' to illustrate Arnold's:
   break-even point
   fixed costs
   total costs
   sales revenue
   area of loss
   margin of safety. (28)

(b) How many desks must he produce and sell in order to break-even?

.... (2)

(c) Assuming fixed costs and variable costs remain the same describe the effect of an increase in sales on the break-even point and area of profit.

....
....
.... (6)

(d) By using calculations or by using your graph, show the effect of variable costs increasing by 12.5%. Indicate clearly:
   (i) how many units would have to be produced and sold to break-even,
   (ii) the sales revenue at break-even.

.... (8)

Fig. 41. Break even exam question.

19
Cash Budgets

Do not confuse a Cash Budget with the Flow of Funds/Sources and Application of Funds described in Chapter 12. Some people call the Flow of Funds Statement a Cash Flow Statement, and this could be confusing. Here you are only concerned with the Cash <u>Budget</u>.

One of the most difficult concepts for students of accounting, and many owners of small businesses, to grasp is that the amount of profit recorded bears no relation at all to the amount of cash the firm actually has. Now that you have worked through this book, you should be able to see why.

- Sales figure includes credit sales, for which money has not yet been received
- The valuation of stock may vary according to the method used. (see chapter on interpretation)
- Amounts deducted from Gross Profit will include depreciation, and provision for bad debts. Both of these are estimated figures.(see chapters 6 & 7).

FORECASTING

There has to be some method of forecasting how much money in cash the business will need. This is absolutely vital, as virtually all businesses need to borrow money. The Bank Manager will want to see a realistic forecast of the business's prospects before he will lend the money. This is useful also in managing household expenses. Six months is usually the most feasible forecast period. You will draw up a chart as shown below.

Suppose Jeremy Green sells about £1000 worth of goods every month. His outgoings are approximately £600 per month for purchases and £300 general expenses. In January he had £300 in cash. His cash budget may now be completed on these (estimated) figures. Although the figures are estimates, they can be fairly accurate if based on past records. His budget, beginning in January, will look like the example below.

Fig 42 Cash budget chart

	Jan	Feb	March	Apr	May	June
Bal at start	300	400	500	600	700	800
+ receipts from sales	1000	1000	1000	1000	1000	1000
	1300	1400	1500	1600	1700	1800
Less expenses	900	900	900	900	900	900
To c/fwd to next month	400	500	600	700	800	900

You will see that Jeremy is going to be in a good position. As long as his sales and expenses remain the same he will have sufficient cash. If, however, his expenses or income had been variable, it would have been a useful way to discover whether Jeremy would need an overdraft or loan.

Try doing a Cash Flow Budget for your own expenses.

Then try this one :

Ivy Houseman owns a boutique. Her cash sales are approximately £2000 per month. She also runs a credit scheme and her sales on this are about £1500 per month.

The debtors (on the credit scheme) always pay during the month following their purchases. Her expenses are approximately £350 a month, wages £500 each month. Draw up her Cash Budget for the next six months, beginning in January.

Now do this question from a 1989 exam paper (Northern Ireland Schools Examination Council Paper 3, question 3 part e.)

Cash Budgets

- Cash budgets are designed to forecast future needs or sufficiency.
- Cash budgets make it possible to play the 'what if' game to help management decisions.

Fig. 43. Cash budget exam question.

(e) Below is Arnold's projected Cash Budget for the first six months of 1990.

RECEIPTS

	Jan	Feb	Mar	Apr	May	June	Total
Sales—Cash	1,000	1,000	1,500	1,500	1,500	1,500	8,000
Sales—Debtors	—	—	500	500	500	500	2,000
Capital	2,000						2,000
Total Receipts	3,000	1,000	2,000	2,000	2,000	2,000	12,000

PAYMENTS

	Jan	Feb	Mar	Apr	May	June	Total
Purchases—Cash	500	1,000	1,000	500	500	500	4,000
Purchases—Creditors	—	—	—	800	600	600	2,000
General Expenses	100	100	400	200	100	100	1,000
Fixtures and Fittings	490	1,500	510	—	—	—	2,500
Wages	300	300	300	300	400	400	2,000
Total Payments	1,390	2,900	2,210	1,800	1,600	1,600	11,500

CASH BUDGET

	Jan	Feb	Mar	Apr	May	June	Total
Opening Balance	—	1,610	(290)	(500)	(300)	100	—
Total Receipts	3,000	1,000	2,000	2,000	2,000	2,000	—
Total Payments	1,390	2,900	2,210	1,800	1,600	1,600	—
Closing Balances	1,610	(290)	(500)	(300)	100	500	—

(i) When is Arnold going to require financial assistance from his bank?
.... (2)

(ii) What would appear to be the principal reason for seeking financial assistance?
.... (2)

(iii) Why do you think there will be no income from Sales Debtors during January and February?
.... (3)

(iv) What change in purchasing pattern occurs from March–April onwards? Give *one* reason for your answer.
....
.... (3)

Summary

- Profit figures do not relate to cash
- Cash budgets are designed to forecast future needs or sufficiency
- Cash budgets make it possible to play the 'what if' game to help management decisions.

Answers to Exercises

These answers are designed to be a learning method. That is why they are fully set out where applicable. If you find them difficult do not despair. Just keep studying the answers and trying to do them again your self.

In some cases notes have been added to help you. Don't forget the more times you do these exercises, the more you are learning. Practise is the very best way to succeed in accounting. Some of the double entry exercises seem very involved. These would actually be easier in a real-life situation.

Many students feel bogged down by double entry bookkeeping. Please don't allow yourself to be discouraged. It is possibly the most tedious section until you have mastered it. Then it becomes very simple and straightforward, If you use a computerised accounting system, the computer will see to all this for you in any case.

In some cases there is more than one way to complete an answer, and the ways shown here are generally the easiest ways.

Chapter 1

Fig 44.

Date	Details	Cash	Bank	Date	Details	Cash	Bank
Jun 1	Bal. b/d	25	30				
Jun 1	Cash sales	30		Jun 2	rent		40.00
	Cheque received		75	Jun 5	goods	10.00	
				Jun 9	phone		50
				Jun 17	window cleaner		5

Fig 45.

Date	Details	Cash	Bank	Date	Details	Cash	Bank
Jun1	Bal. b/d	5	30	Jun 6	rent		35
Jun 3	Cheque received		10	Jun 10	wages	20	
				Jun 12	paid out		40
Jun5	Cash sales	25					
Jun6	Cash sales	10					
Jun 12	Cash sales	20					
	Cash sales		35		To c/d	40	
	To c/d	60	75			60	75
	Bal b/d	40			Bal B/d		35

Chapter 1 continued
Fig 46 Gemma's cash book

DATE	DETAILS	Discount	CASH	BANK	DATE	DETAILS	Discount	CASH	BANK
July 1	Balance b/d		40		July 1	Balance b/d		35	
2	Cheque received	2		38	15	Paid supplier	1·25		23·75
4	Cash sales paid into bank			30	25	Paid cleaner		20	
20	Cash sales		10			Balances c/d		30	9·25
		2	50	68			1·25	50	68·00
	Balances b/d		30	9·25					

Fig. 47
Cash Book of Mourne Enterprises

Date	Details	Discount	Cash	Bank	Date	Details	Discount	Cash	Bank
Mar 1	Balance B/d		50	2,400	Mar 1	Balance B/d			1,150
2	Sales			540	3	Cleaners		28	
4	W. Scott	5	400		3	P. Murphy			1,000
4	Bank (contra)				4	Cash (contra)			400
					5	Salaries			480
					5	Balance c/d		62	310
		5	90	2,940				90	2,940
Mar 6	Balance B/d		62	310					

Other answers:

c. Cash in hand now £62. Firm now has £310 in its bank account – no longer an overdraft.
d. To encourage prompt payment of invoices
e. Transfer of funds from cash to bank or vice-versa

Chapter 2

Fig 48
John Moss

Cash Book

Date	Details	Cash	Bank	Date	Details	Cash	Bank
	Bal B/d	50.00	500.00				
	Sales	515.00			Purchases		350.00
					Rent	20.00	
					Equipment		150.00
					petrol	50.00	
					C/d	495.00	
		565.00	500.00			565.00	500.00

Bal B/d   495.00

As the bank columns are the same, there is nothing to c/d there.

Purchases

Date	Details	Dr	Cr	Balance
	Bal B/d			250.00
	Produce	350.00		500.00

Sales

Date	Details	Dr	Cr	Balance
	Bal B/d			320.00cr
	Cash		515.00	835.00cr

Rent

Date	Details	Dr	Cr	Balance
	Bal B/d			20.00
	Cash	20.00		40.00

Equipment

Date	Details	Dr	Cr	Balance
	Scales (bank)	150.00		150.00

Petrol

Date	Details	Dr	Cr	Balance
	Cash	50.00		50.00

Fig 49
Mandy Baxter

Date	Details	Cash	Bank	Date	Details	Cash	Bank
	Capital		5500.00		Equipment		60.00
	Bank	100.00c			Cash		100.00c
	Cash sales	2350.00			Fixtures		1500.00
	cash		2350.00c		Rent		1200.00
					Bank	2350.00c	
					virgo		2450.00
					Bal c/d	100.00	2540.00
		2450.00	7850.00			2450.00	7850.00

Bal b/d   100.00   2540.00

Capital

Date	Details	Dr	Cr	Balance
	Bank		5500.00	5500.00cr

Equipment

Date	Details	Dr	Cr	Balance
	Till (bank)	60.00		60.00

Fixtures

Date	Details	Dr	Cr	Balance
	Bank	1500.00		1500.00

Virgo Clothing

Date	Details	Dr	Cr	Balance
	Stock of clothing		2450.00	2450.00
	paid	2450.00		0.00

Purchases

Date	Details	Dr	Cr	Balance
	Virgo	2450.00		2450.00

Sales

Date	Details	Dr	Cr	Balance
	Cash		2350.00	2350.00cr

Rent

Date	Details	Dr	Cr	Balance
	Bank	1200.00		1200.00

Notes on Mandy Baxter

Note that when she paid Virgo Clothing the entry was
Credit the cash book and debit Virgo Clothing.
This brings the account to nil.

The purchase on credit was still entered in the purchases account. The Virgo account replaced the cash book entry temporarily. Then, when she paid Virgo, the amount was cleared from their account and was entered in the cash book.

All sales and purchases (for re-sale) are entered in the sales and purchases accounts respectively, whether they are paid for immediately or not.

If you had entered the till in the fixtures and fittings account, rather than equipment, this would be acceptable. Different firms have their own ways, and names for their accounts.

Fig 50
Harry Webster

Date	Details	Cash	Bank	Date	Details	Cash	Bank
Oct1	Capital		5000	Oct 2	Machinery		2650
Oct 4	Sales	23		Oct 8	Alpha		100
Oct 8	Sales	50			Bal c/d	73	2250
		73	5000			73	2250
	Bal b/d	73	2250				

Capital

Date	Details	Dr	Cr	Balance
	Bank		5000.00	5000.00cr

Machinery

Date	Details	Dr	Cr	Balance
	Bank	2650		2650

Purchases

Date	Details	Dr	Cr	Balance
	Alpha	100		100
	Alpha	75		175

Alpha Products

Date	Details	Dr	Cr	Balance
	Purchases		100	100cr
	Purchases		75	175cr
	Bank	100		75cr

Balfour bell

Date	Details	Dr	Cr	Balance
	Sales	55		55

Sales

Date	Details	Dr	Cr	Balance
	Balfour Bell		55	55cr
	Silverman		72	127cr
	Cash		23	150cr
	Cash		50	200cr

Silverman Ins.

Date	Details	Dr	Cr	Balance
	Sales	72		72

Fig 51
Mary Martin

Date	Details	Cash	Bank	Date	Details	Cash	Bank
	Capital		6200		Touchwood Enterprises		2300
	Cash sale	73.56			Rent		100
					Window cleaner	5.00	
					Drawings	25.00	
					Bal c/d	43.56	3800
		73.56	6200			73.56	6200
	Bal b/d	43.56	3800				

Capital (Nominal Ledger)

Date	Details	Dr	Cr	Balance
	Bank		6200	6200cr

Equipment (Nominal Ledger)

Date	Details	Dr	Cr	Balance
	Bank	2300		2300

Sales Day Book

Date	Details	Invoice Amount	VAT	Total
	A. South	50	8.75	58.75
	A. South	45	7.88	52.88
	M. Sugden	50	8.75	58.75
		145	25.38	

Sales Returns Day Book

Details	Invoice Amount	VAT	Total
M. Sugden	12.50	2.19	14.69

Purchases Day Book

Date	Details	Invoice Amount	VAT	Total
	Paper Path	200	35	235
	Paper Path	75	13.13	88.13
		275	48.13	

Purchase Returns Day Book

Details	Credit note amount	VAT	Total
Paper Path	25	4.38	29.38

Fig 52. Mary Martin (continued)

Rent (Nominal Ledger)

Date	Details	Dr	Cr	Balance
	Bank	100		100

Cleaning (Nominal Ledger)

Date	Details	Dr	Cr	Balance
	Window Cleaner	5		5

Paper Path (Purchase Ledger)

Date	Details	Dr	Cr	Balance
	Purchase Day Book		235	235cr
	Purchase Day Book		88.13	323.13cr
	Returns	29.33		293.75cr

A South (Sales Ledger)

Date	Details	Dr	Cr	Balance
	Sales Day Book	58.75		58.75
	Sales Day Book	52.88		111.63

Drawings (Nominal Ledger)

Date	Details	Dr	Cr	Balance
	Cash	25		25

M.Sugden (Sales Ledger)

Date	Details	Dr	Cr	Balance
	Sales	58.75		58.75
	Returns		14.69	44.06

Purchase Returns (Nominal)

Date	Details	Dr	Cr	Balance
	Paper Path		25	25cr

Sales Returns (Nominal)

Date	Details	Dr	Cr	Balance
	M.Sugden	12.50		12.50

VAT (Nominal)

Date	Details	Dr	Cr	Balance
	Purchase Returns		4.38	4.38cr
	Sales D.Book total		25.38	29.76cr
	Purch. D.B. total	48.13		18.37
	Sales returns	2.19		20.56
	Cash Sale		10.96	9.60

Sales (Nominal)

Date	Details	Dr	Cr	Balance
	Cash		62.60	62.60cr
	Sales D. Book total		145.00	207.60cr

Purchases (Nominal)

Date	Details	Dr	Cr	Balance
	Purch.D.Bk.Total	275		275

Note: VAT here is calculated at 17.5%

Fig.53
J.Glendenning.

J.Harryot

Date	Details	Dr	Cr	Bal
Aug 1	Balance			500cr
4	Purchases		1400	1900cr
10	Returns	96		1804cr
14	Cheque	450		1354cr
	Discount	50		1304cr
28	Error on discount		25	1329cr
Sep 1	Balance			1329cr

K.Fellowes

Date	Details	Dr	Cr	Bal
Aug 1	Balance			670cr
5	Purchases		890	1560cr
19	Credit note	40		1520cr
Sep 1	Balance			1520cr

Note: If these were your own books, you would not need to repeat the balance at Sept 1st

If you are doing an exam which calls for you to show the balance at a particular date, it is best to do this as above.

Chapter 3

Harry Webster's total balance totals 5275.

Spotting errors in the trial balance

Commission
Original entry
Omission
Reversal of entries
Principle
Compensating

Exam Question

1. A trial balance is a list of balances taken from the accounts in a double entry book-keeping system.
2. The purpose is to test the arithmetical accuracy of the book-keeping.
3. The balance sheet is a statement of affairs of the company. The trial balance is simply a listing of figures on the debit and credit sides as a spot check for any errors.
4. Any four of the six listed above, 1-6.
5. None of them would upset the balance between debits and credits. Refer to the chapter and give a detailed explanation of two of them.
6. Use any four examples from the first question of this chapter, which asked you to name the type of error.
7. a).Equal value: this could mean that one half of a double entry has been missed off, or something may be included in the records which shouldn't be there.

    b)Half the difference: this would mean that an item could have been debited instead of credited, or vice versa. For this reason it would also be advisable to look for items of twice the value.

Chapter 4

B.Burton's Account
B.Burton Trading And Profit And Loss Account For Year Ended...

Sales		1000
Opening Stock	2950	
Purchases	4850	
	7800	
Closing stock	3270	
		4530
Gross Profit		5470
Expenses		
Travelling expenses	420	
Administration exp.	310	
Electricity	500	
		1230
Net Profit		4240

N.Iveson's Account
N.Iveson's Trading and Profit and Loss Account for the year ended...

Sales		15000
Opening Stock	4500	
Purchases	21000	
	25500	
Closing Stock	3200	
		22300
Gross Loss		(7300)
Expenses		500
Net Loss		(7800)

You will see that the result is not always a profit. Note also that accountants put figures in **brackets** to denote a **minus** figure.

N.Carter's Account
Nathan Carter Trading and Profit and Loss Account for the year ended..

Sales			25713
Less returns inward			235
			25478
Opening Stock		10000	
Purchases	19642		
Add carriage inwards	242		
	19884		
Less returns outward	150		
		19734	
		29734	
Less closing stock		14000	
			15734
Gross Profit			9744
Expenses:			
Salaries	4214		
Admin. Expenses	2231		
Rent	3210		
			9655
Net Profit			89

J. Baker Trading and Profit and Loss Account for the quarter ended
31 Dec 1988

Sales			37000
Less returns inward			250
			36750
Opening Stock		5000	
Purchases	25000		
Add carriage inwards	750		
	25750		
Less returns outward	900		
		24850	
		29850	
Less closing stock		4500	
			25350
			11400
Wages (trading account)			9500
Gross Profit			1900
Expenses:			
Carriage outwards	1050		
Selling expenses	750		
			1800
Net Profit			100

Profit adjustments
a. −
b. +
c. −
d. + because you would enter the profit and loss account from the rent account.

Exam Question

Answer given in chapter
−620
+680
+10000 (adjust purchases!)
−300
+400

N.Barlow's account
Trading and Profit and Loss Account for N Barlow for the year ended …(date)

Sales			23000
Opening Stock	7500		
Purchases	15000		
	22500		
Less closing stock	5500		
Cost of Sales			17000
Gross Profit			6000
Insurance	800		
Less in advance	200		
		600	
Electricity	650		
Last year's	150		
		500	
Administration		2300	
Wages/salaries		16000	
			19400
Net Loss			(13400)

Note that both prepayment and accrual are deducted, as neither of them belongs to this year.
If owing for *this* year, it would be added on.

Chapter 5

B. Bertram Balance Sheet as at …

Fixed Assets		
Premises		28000
Van		5000
		33000
Current Assets		
Stock	4000	
Debtors	2500	
Bank	1000	
	7500	
Current Liabilities		
Creditors	3000	
		4500
Net Worth		37500
Financed by		
Capital	30000	
Add Net Profit	8000	
	38000	
Less drawings	500	
		37500

G. Cooper Profit and Loss Account for the year ended…

Sales		40000
Purchases	30000	
Less closing stock	10000	
Cost of Sales		20000
Gross Profit		20000
Expenses		
Insurance	500	
Wages	5000	
Rates	3000	
Electricity	2000	
		10500
Net profit		9500

G. Cooper Balance Sheet as at....

Fixed Assets			
Premises			30000
Fittings			5000
Van			6500
			41500
Current Assets			
Stock	10000		
Debtors	7000		
Bank	10000		
		27000	
Current Liabilities			
Creditors		4000	
			2300
Net Worth			64500
Financed by			
Capital	59000		
Add Net Profit	9500		
		68500	
Less drawings		4000	
			64500

Jason Green Balance Sheet as at 31st May 1989

Fixed Assets			
Premises			60000
Fixtures and Fittings			12000
			72000
Current Assets			
Stock	15000		
Debtors	4000		
Cash	200		
Prepaid expenses	800		
		20000	
Current Liabilities			
Expense creditors	580		
Trade creditors	2000		
Bank overdraft	1420		
		4000	
Working capital			16000
			88000
Long term liabilities			
Mortgage on premises			6000
Net Worth			82000
Financed by			
Capital			89000
Less drawings	6000		
And Net loss	1000		
			7000
			82000

Note that the amount prepaid by Jason is a current asset.
The bank overdraft is a current liability. The definition of a current liability is anything falling due within one year. A bank overdraft, in theory, can be called in at any time, and so is classed as a current liability.

Chapter 6

Straight line: 1450
Reducing balance: 1500, 1275, 1084
Revaluation: 35

Fig.54
Z & G Castings

Provision for depreciation

	Dr	Cr	Bal
Yr 1		600	600
Yr 2		480	1080
Yr 3		384	1464

OR

	Dr	Cr
Yr 1		600
Yr 2		480
Yr 3		384
Bal to c/d	1464	
totals	1464	1464
Bal b/d		1464

Balance sheet Extracts:

		Cost	Acc.dep.	Net
Yr 1	Machine	3000	600	2400
Yr 2	Machine	3000	1080	1920
Yr 3	Machine	3000	1464	1536

AB Engineering

Balance sheet extracts:

		Cost	Acc.dep.	Net
Yr 1	Machine	20000	2000	18000
Yr 2	Machine	20000	4000	16000
Yr 3	Machine	20000	6000	14000

In Profit and Loss account:

Yr 1	2000
Yr 2	2000
Yr 3	2000

Chapter 7

Note: Amounts for B.Taggart are rounded to the nearest pound.

Fig.55
B. Taggart

Bad debts account

Date	Details	Dr	Cr	Bal
	Written off accounts	750		750

Provision for bad debts

Date	Details	Dr	Cr	Bal
	(7% of 5000)		350	350

Profit and Loss account figures:
Debit 750
Debit 350
(debit in profit and loss account means it will be deducted).

Balance sheet entry:
Current Assets

Debtors	5000	
Less prov for bad debts	350	
		4650

Fig.56
M.Bedwin
Provision for bad debts

Date	Details	Dr	Cr	Bal
1988			181.50	181.50
1989			54.50	236.00
1990			61.00	297.00

Profit and loss account:
dr.181.50
dr. 54.50
dr. 61.00

Balance Sheet Extracts:

1988	Debtors	3630.00	
	Less provision for bad debts	181.50	
			3448.50
1989	Debtors	4720.00	
	Less provision for bad debts	236.00	
			4484.00
1990	Debtors	5940.00	
	Less provision for bad debts	297.00	
			5643.00

Fig. 57

M.Cox
Bad debts

Date	Details	Dr	Cr	Bal
1989		326		326

Provision for bad debts

Date	Details	Dr	Cr	Bal
1989			491	491
1990			71	562

Profit and loss account entries

1989	dr	491
1989	dr	326
1990	dr	71

Balance sheet extracts

1988	Debtors		3226
1989	debtors	4914	
		491	
			4423
1990	Debtors	5620.00	
		562.00	
			5058

Chapter 8

Working out the types of cost
Prime
Prime
Prime
Production
Production
Production
Prime
Production
Production
Production

A manufacturing account

Stock of raw materials at start	650	
+ purchases	<u>1000</u>	
		1650
Less raw materials at end		<u>700</u>
Cost of raw materials consumed		950
Direct wages	3000	
Royalties	<u>300</u>	
		3300
Prime cost		4250
Factory overheads		
Rent	900	
Depreciation	400	
Maintenance wages	2000	
Parts for repairs	<u>100</u>	
		<u>3400</u>
Production cost of completed goods		7650

167

B.Best's Account
Manufacturing and trading and profit and loss account for B.Best for the year ended…

Stock of raw materials at start		3000
Purchases	9000	
+ carriage	500	
		9500
		12500
Less raw materials at end		4000
Cost of raw materials consumed		8500
Direct wages		7000
Prime cost		15500
Factory expenses	3000	
Canteen expenses	1000	
		4000
Production cost of finished goods		19500
Sales		40000
Opening stock of finished goods	5000	
Production cost of finished goods	19500	
	24500	
Closing stock of finished goods	3500	
Cost of Sales		21000
Gross profit		19000
Administration expenses	6000	
Selling and distribution expenses	7500	
Depreciation of office equipment	500	
Provision for bad debts	350	
		14350
Net profit		4650

Chapter 9

Income and Expenditure Account for the Wolds Way Rambling Club for the year ended…

Workings

Trading account for refreshments		
Sale of refreshments		15
Refreshments at start	12	
Purchases	<u>7</u>	
	19	
Refreshments at end	<u>10</u>	
		<u>9</u>
Gross profit on refreshments		6

Income
Subs received 250
Profit on refreshments 6
Rucksacks sold 350
Rucksacks bought <u>200</u>
 150
Income from coffee morning <u>65</u>
Total Income 471

Expenditure
Fees for speaker 25
Rent for village halls <u>35</u>
 <u>60</u>
Surplus of income over expenditure <u>411</u>

Radcliffe Social Club.

Receipts and Payments Account for the year ended 31 December 1988

Receipts	Payments
b/d 890	670
3200	2500
46000	860
	38500
	To c/d 7560
50090	50090
b/d 7560	

Income and Expenditure Account for the year ended 31 December 1988

Income

Subs 3200-150 next years	3050	
Admissions	46000	
		49050
Expenditure		
Rates	670	
Lighting and heating 860+90 owing	950	
Fees paid	38500	
		40120
Surplus of income over expenditure		8930

Note: although £5000 was incurred during the period, £2500 of this is classed as a short term loan, and will therefore appear in the balance sheet as a current liability rather than be deducted as expenditure. The notes said that it was repayable within one year so it will be *next* year's account.

Balance Sheet as at 31 December 1988

Fixed Assets			
Furniture			5000
Current Assets			
Bank		7560	
Current Liabilities			
Subs in advance	150		
Short term loan (furniture)	2500		
Electricity bill owing	<u>90</u>		
		<u>2740</u>	
			<u>4820</u>
Net Assets (Net worth)			<u>9820</u>
Financed by:			
Cash at start		890	
+surplus		<u>8930</u>	
			<u>9820</u>

Chapter 10

Appropriation Account Exercise
Partnership appropriation account of Green, Cross and Bowles

Net Profit		35000
Interest on drawings: Green	600	
Cross	400	
Bowles	400	
		1400
		36400
Salary for Green		12000
		24400
Interest on capital: Green	400	
Cross	500	
Bowles	500	
		1400
		23000
Share of Profit: Green	4600	
Cross	9200	
Bowles	9200	
		23000

An exam question:
- Drawings are money taken out of the business by the owner(s) for his/their own use.

- Interest on drawings is money charged to the owner(s) on the drawings taken out. It discourages the taking of too much in drawings.

- Provision for depreciation is an amount calculated to set against the value of assets. The purpose is to avoid overstating the profits or worth of the business.

- Working capital is calculated by deducting current liabilities from current assets. It is the liquid asset amount which is in constant flux within the business.

- Interest on capital is the amount the business pays to the owner(s) on the amount of capital he/they have put into the business.

Fig.58.
Bunker and Lake Profit and Loss Appropriation Account for the year ended 31 December 1988

Net trading profit		40600
Interest on drawings:		
Bunker	400	
Lake	1800	
		2200
		42800
Interest on capital:		
Bunker (40000 x 8%)	3200	
Lake (50000 x 8%)	4000	
		7200
		35600
Share of profits:		
Bunker	17800	
Lake	17800	
		35600

Current Accounts
Bunker

Details	Dr	Cr	Bal
Balance			8400cr
Drawings	24000		15600
Interest on drawings	400		16000
Interest on capital		3200	12800
Share of profit		17800	5000cr

OR alternatively:

	Dr	Cr
Bal		8400
Drawings	24000	
Interest on drawings	400	
Interest on capital		3200
Share of profit		17800
Bal to c/d	5000	
	29400	29400
Bal b/d		5000

Lake

Details	Dr	Cr	Bal
Balance			4120
Drawings	30000		34120
Interest on drawings	1800		35920
Interest on capital		4000	31920
Share of profit		17800	14120

OR alternatively:

	Dr	Cr
Bal	4120	
Drawings	30000	
Interest on drawings	1800	
Interest on capital		4000
Share of profit		17800
Bal to c/d		14120
	35920	35920
Bal b/d	14120	

Balance Sheet for Bunker and Lake as at 31 December 1988

Fixed Assets	Cost	Accumulated Depreciation	Net
Premises	100000	-	100000
Motor Van	12000	9000	3000
	112000	9000	103000

Current Assets			
Debtors	6420		
Bank	6596		
		13016	
Current Liabilities			
Wages accrued	3936		
Interest owing	1200		
		5136	
			7880
Net assets			110880
Less long term loan			30000
			80880

Financed by:
    Partners' capital accounts:

Bunker	40000	
Lake	50000	
		90000
+credit current account Bunker		5000
		95000
Less debit current account Lake		14120
		80880

Note: Current accounts, like the capital account, are usually credit balances. They represent what the business owes to the partner. In this case Lake has a debit balance. This represents what he owes to the business.

Chapter 11

N. Rose & Co.
Required for distribution:
75000 x 8% preference shares = 6000
100000 x 12% ordinary shares = <u>12000</u>
                                18000

An exam question

Streamline Plc Profit and Loss Appropriation Account for the year ended 31 December 1990

Profit and Loss b/fwd		34000
Net profit for year		<u>15000</u>
		49000
Transfer to general reserve		<u>20000</u>
		29000
Preference share dividend	1000	
Ordinary share dividend	<u>18000</u>	
		<u>19000</u>
Unappropriated profit		10000

Balance Sheet as at 31 December 1990

Fixed Assets	Cost	Accumulated Depreciation	Net
Premises	250000	-	250000
Plant & machinery	140000	50000	90000
			340000

Current Assets			
Stock	16540		
Debtors	12080		
Bank	15280		
Prepaid advertising	2000		
		45900	

Current Liabilities			
Creditors	3000		
Wages owing	3900		
Proposed dividend	19000		
		25900	
			20000
Net worth			360000

Financed by:

Authorised share capital		520000
Issued share capital:		
Ordinary shares	300000	
Preference shares	20000	
		320000
General reserve + new	30000	
Unappropriated profit	10000	
		40000
		360000

Chapter 12

An exam question

a) Criticism in this instance means appraisal of contents.

Forge Engineering:
Has a more valuable premises (by 20000)
Has more machinery (by 10000)
Has more money owing to it by debtors (by 6200)
Has stock which is depreciating
Has a greater amount of share capital
Has almost twice as much undistributed profit as Metal Products
Has a large bank overdraft (whereas Metal Products has a bank balance of £200)
Owes £6000 more to its creditors than Metal Products does

b) Previous year's balance sheet and profit and loss account for both years would be useful, then it would be possible to also do a flow of funds.

c) Accounting ratios: e.g. current ratio, acid test ratio, working capital. You are limited owing to the lack of information available.

d) The Metal Products Ltd is in a good position of liquidity and could be safely taken over, although it would be desirable to have the necessary figures to calculate the profitability ratio:

$$\frac{\text{net profit}}{\text{Sales}} \times 100 = \% \text{ profitability}$$

The other firm, Forge Engineering, is not such a good proposition. Not only is it in a poor state of liquidity, but also has a large bank overdraft.

Note: It is purely a matter of opinion which firm (if either) to take over. This is one of those questions with no right or wrong answer. It is a matter of considering all points.

Chapter 13

Practise sheet for flow of funds statement (1)
KS Alarms
Sources of funds

Increase in creditors	6800	
Net profit	9700	
Loan	4000	
		20500 |//
Application of funds		
Increase in fixed assets	20000	
Increase in stock	5000	
Increase in debtors	2500	
		27500
Excess of application over sources		(7000)
Proof:		
Cash at start		12000
Cash at end		5000
Cash used		7000

Practise sheet for flow of funds statement (2)
J Bird
Sources of funds

Increase in creditors	700	
Net profit	14500	
		15200
Application of funds		
Increase in fixed assets	10000	
Increase in stock	1650	
Increase in debtors	2300	
Drawings	4750	
		18700
Excess of application over sources		(3500)
Proof:		
Bank at start	2000	
Bank at end o/d	1500	
Cash used		3500

Chapter 14

Alfred Smith's business
Trading and Profit and Loss Account for the year ended...

Sales = total of invoices sent		744
+ cash received		<u>53</u>
		797
Opening stock	490	
Purchases	<u>352</u>	
	842	
Closing stock	<u>350</u>	
Cost of sales		<u>492</u>
Gross Profit		305
Expenses		<u>178</u>
Net profit		127

Balance sheet as at......
Current assets

Stock	350
Debtors	744
Bank	<u>976</u>
Net assets	2070
Financed By:	
Capital at start	?
Net profit	<u>127</u>
	<u>2070</u>

Here you have to deduce that the capital start was £1943. Note that balance sheets do not always look quite as you might expect!

Chapter 15

Will Grant's account

Sales		3300
Opening stock	3200	
Purchases	2600	
	5800	
Closing stock	3600	
Cost of sales		2200
Gross profit		1100

It is easier to work the whole thing out if you do a trading account as above. Just leave blanks at first where the figures are unknown. You can fill them in as you go:

First find the closing stock: 3400 x 2 – 3200 = 3600
Now you will be able to do the cost of sales
If mark up is 50% then the profit must be 50% of cost, so it is 50% of 2200 = 1100.
You know that if mark up is 50% then margin will be $33^{1/3}$% so profit must be 1/3 of sales. So sales are 3 times profit =3300.

An exam question

Stock value at 4th June	7600
Less purchases	840
	6760
Add sales (see workings)	880
	7640
Less return	48
	7592
Add drawn	30
Corrected net profit	7622

Workings:
Takings at tills   820
Add credit sales   280
                  1100
Mark up = 25% (1/4) so margin on sales is 20% (1/5)
1100 less 20% =880
60 less 20% = 48

Chapter 16

Exercise in reconciling
Corrected cash book balance

Balance	315
Add standing order	37
	352
Less charges	10
Corrected cash book balance	342

Bank reconciliation

Bank statement balance	114
Add cheques not credited:	
K.Petty	106
C.Ashton	92
G.Robin	62
	374
Less cheque paid out	32
Real balance	342

An exam question

1. Any three of the following:
    Credit transfer (26.89)
    Standing order (93.56)
    Bank charges (18.50)
    Unpresented cheque (12.67)
    Cheque not credited (210.50)

2. Cheques are not presented to the bank for payment in the same order that you enter them.

3. Bank Account

Bal b/d	524.27	Standing order	93.56
Credit transfer	26.89	Bank charges	18.50
		Bal to c/d	439.10
	551.16		551.16
Bal b/d	439.10		

Fig 59

Bank Reconciliation Statement

Balance as bank statement	241.27
Add cheques not credited	<u>210.50</u>
	451.77
Less cheques not presented	<u>12.67</u>
Balance	439.10

Last question: Four of the same reasons as in part 1 above.

Chapter 17

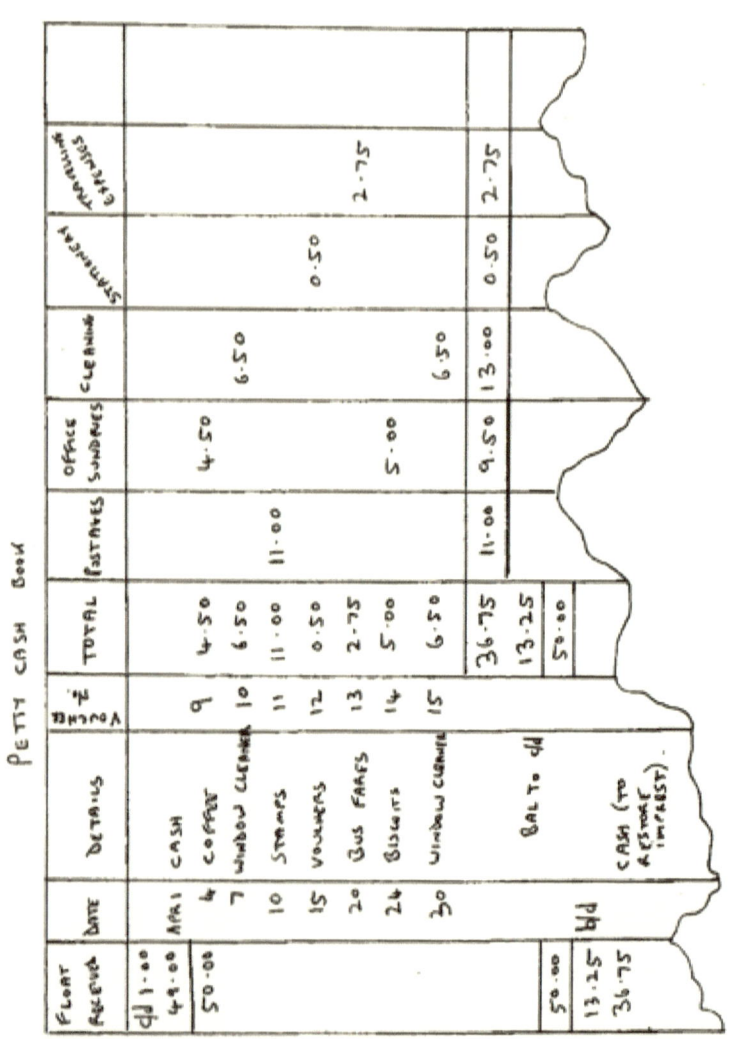

Fig.60

An exam question
a. Brian has petty cash vouchers with the signatures of the people to whom he has given money.

An exam question
a. Brian has petty cash vouchers with the signatures of the people to whom he has given money.

Receipts	Date	Details	Voucher Number	Total Payments	Cleaning	Postage	Travelling Expenses
25.00	Sep 8	Balance					
	8	Bus Fares	85	0.60			0.60
	8	Postage	86	3.40		3.40	
	9	W. Cleaner	87	4.00	4.00		
	10	Taxi	88	3.00			3.00
	10	Rail Fare	89	10.00			10.00
	12	Stamps	90	2.10		2.10	
				23.10	4.00	5.50	13.60
		Bal to c/d →		1.90			
25	00			25.00			
1	90	Bal b/d					
23	10	Bal given to restore imprest					

Fig 61

Chapter 18

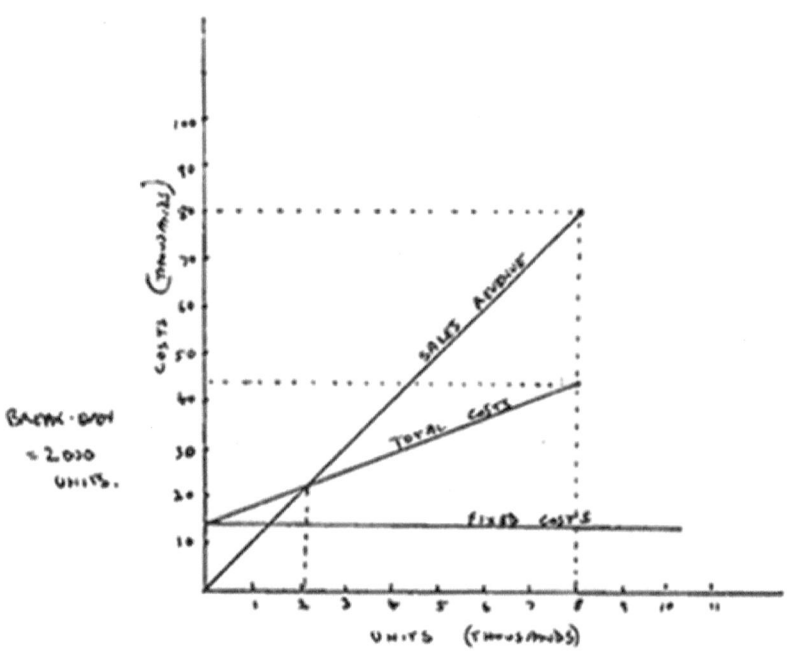

Fig 62

To plot sales revenue:-
Exp. Sales x rev = 8000 x (price per unit) £10 = 80000
Plot from 8000(exp.sales) to 80000 costs and draw line from 0 to this point.

To plot total costs:-
(var.costs x exp.sales) + fixed costs = (£4 x 8000)+ 12000 = 44000
Plot from exp. Sales (8000 units) to 44000. Draw line from fixed costs to this point.

An exam question

a. Break Even Graph

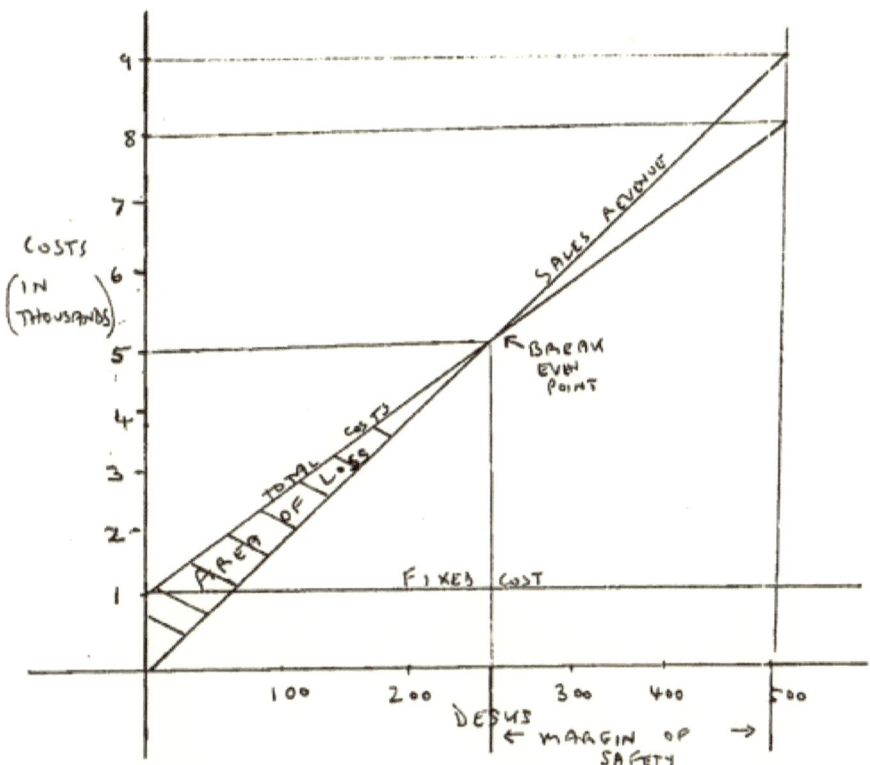

Fig 63

Fixed costs = 1000
Total costs = 9000
Sales revenue = 1000
Margin = £4 per desk
Sales revenue at break even = 5000

b. 250 desks

c. Break even point will remain constant, but the area of profit will be larger.

Note: you could draw a rough version of your graph to prove this to yourself. However, if you have understood the principles, this answer should be obvious to you.

d. Formula =

$$\frac{\text{Fixed costs}}{\text{Selling price} - \text{variable costs}} = \frac{1000}{20-16}$$

Now = $\frac{1000}{20-18 \ (16+12.5\%)}$

= $\frac{1000}{2}$

Answer = 500 units
Sales revenue at break even = 500 x £20 = £10000

Chapter 19

Cash Budget for Ivy Houseman

	Jan	Feb	Mar	Apr	May	Jun
Balance at start	-	1150	3800	6450	9100	11750
Receipts	2000	3500	3500	3500	3500	3500
	2000	4650	7300	9950	12600	15250
Expenses	850	850	850	850	850	850
Balance at end	1150	3800	6450	9100	11750	14400

Fig. 64

An exam question
i. Arnold will need financial assistance in February, March and April.
ii. The main reason seems to be purchase of fixtures and fittings.
iii. No income from debtors for first two months as two months' credit is allowed.
iv. Less cash purchases; more credit purchases.

Reasons : less resources. Probably one month credit allowed. More income from debtors.

Accounting Concepts

Accounting entity

(Or sometimes called **Business entity**) The fact that the business is a separate entity. It is separate from the owner. The owner must therefore have a separate bank account for his private use.

Accruals (matching)

The need to compare income and expenditure over the same period they were *incurred* not paid.

Consistency

Whatever accounting method is chosen, e.g. types of depreciation, the same method must continue to be used from year to year,

Continuity
(Or **going concern**). The assumption that the business will continue to trade.

Duality

Double entry. There is always another half to every entry, one debit and one credit.

Materiality

The way in which relatively small items are treated in the accounts, ie common sense prevails.

Money measurement

Transactions are always written up as amounts in money, but you need to be aware that it does not necessarily refer to the amount of cash in the business.

Prudence (conservatism)

The accountant always accounts for possible losses, but never overstates profits: cautious attitude.

Glossary

A/c. Abbreviation for account.

Account. A record of debits and credits which shows how much is owed.

Asset. Something owned by the business, eg premises, or an amount in favour of the business, eg rent paid in advance by the business. Includes anything owing to business.

Accounting concept. A rule of accountancy. There are many of these. The ones you need to know are listed in this book with explanations (see Contents).

Annum. Year.

Appropriation. Sharing out, distributing profits.

b/d. An abbreviation for **brought down**. It refers to the balance or amount left with which to continue the account.

B/fwd. An abbreviation for **brought forward**. Exactly the same as b/d. Either abbreviation may be used.

Balance. The amount on an account; the amount needed to close an account. To balance the books means to have everything correct and in agreement.

Book of original entry. The place where any transaction is first recorded. It is not usually part of the accounting system, just a record. The **cash book** is the exception as it is part of the system and also a book or original entry.

c/d. An abbreviation for **carried down**. It is written against the amount which will still be left on the account. Sometimes written as 'To c/d'.

C/fwd. Exactly the same as c/d. Either abbreviation may be used.

Capital. The amount of money the owner(s) put into the business. What the business owes the owner(s).

Capital employed. The total amount of capital plus net profit less drawings. It should be the same as net worth (see chapters on balance sheet and interpretation of final accounts).

Concept. In accounting terms this is one of the rules (see **accounting concept** above).

Credit. All transactions are said to be either debit or credit. To credit someone's account means that you owe them or they have paid you.

Debit. Loosely, this is something which is owned by or owed to the business. Note that debit and credit in accounting are different from the account you have with your bank.

Dishonoured cheque. A cheque which is returned when you have paid it into the bank. This will be for one of several reasons such as insufficient funds in drawer's account, no signature, not written out correctly and so on.

Drawer. The person on whose account a cheque will be drawn, ie the person who signed it, or the firm whose name appears under the signature.

Final accounts. Trading and profit and loss accounts, balance sheets.

Imprest. Float: amount of money kept in petty cash. Name given to system used for petty cash.

Liability. An expense or debt incurred by the business. Something that is owed by the business. Net **or** nett. The final amount when all expenses/deductions have
been made.

Payee. The person or firm to whom a cheque is made out— the recipient.

Posting. A term used in accounting to describe entering amounts on to the accounts.

Reconciliation. The act of making two things agree. The statement from the bank has to be reconciled with your own record.
The purchase ledger accounts will have to be reconciled against the bills/demands/statements you get from suppliers.

Refer to drawer. This phrase of r/d will be stamped on a dishonoured cheque by the bank.

Revenue. Money. Sales revenue is money generated from sales. Revenue expenses are the regular yearly expenses.

Transaction. The act of selling or buying something.

Unpresented cheque. A cheque you have paid out, but which has not yet appeared on your bank statement.

Working capital. Current assets less current liabilities (see chapter on the balance sheet for explanation of these).

Index

accrued expenses, 53
Acid test, 104
Analysis Cash Book, 16
appropriation account, 85, 86, 98, 172
Articles of Association, 95
asset, 19, 38, 42, 46, 55, 58, 60, 61, 65, 66, 67, 68, 69, 82, 101, 104, 162, 172
authorised share capital, 95, 97, 98, 99, 100
AVCO, 107
bad debts account., 69
balance sheet, 4, 55, 57, 58, 60, 63, 64, 65, 67, 71, 72, 83, 93, 99, 101, 102, 103, 108, 155, 170, 178, 192, 193
Bank Reconciliation, 123
bankrupt, 69, 85, 94
book of original entry, 7, 32
Break Even Analysis, 135
break even point, 135
Business Entity, 18, 23
Called Up Capital, 96
capital account, 18, 26, 89, 92, 175
Capital account, 27
Capital Allowances, 62
Capital expenditure, 58
Carriage inwards, 48
Carriage outwards, 48
cash book, 4, 7, 8, 9, 10, 11, 12, 13, 14, 15, 16, 17, 18, 19, 20, 22, 23, 24, 27, 52, 113, 115, 123, 124, 125, 126, 127, 129, 130, 131, 132, 144, 149, 182, 191
Cash Budget, 139
certificate of incorporation., 95
closing stock, 46
Commission (Misposting, 42
Compensating, 42, 155
contra entry, 16, 22
credit, 7, 8, 14, 15, 18, 19, 20, 22, 24, 25, 28, 30, 35, 36, 37, 39, 70, 82, 89, 92, 113, 114, 122, 126, 139, 140, 155, 175, 181, 189, 190, 192
current account, 89, 93, 175
Current Assets, 55, 56, 64, 71, 72, 99, 101, 102, 109, 111, 112, 116, 160, 161, 162, 165, 171, 175, 177
Current ratio, 103
debentures, 97
debit, 7, 8, 10, 14, 15, 18, 19, 20, 22, 24, 39, 41, 70, 92, 126, 155, 165, 175, 190, 192
deficit, 80

depreciation, 4, 60, 61, 62, 63, 64, 65, 66, 67, 68, 92, 93, 100, 101, 102, 106, 139, 163, 172, 190
Depreciation Account, 66
discount, 13, 15, 16, 37, 154
discounts allowed, 13
discounts received, 13
disposal account, 68
dividends, 95
double entry, 18, 19, 22, 23, 24, 30, 34, 41, 52, 68, 70, 113, 142, 155
Double entry, 4, 18, 25, 190
drawings, 84
Duality Accounting concept, 23
Factory Overheads, 76
FIFO, 107
Fixed Assets, 55, 56, 64, 65, 99, 101, 102, 109, 111, 112, 116, 160, 161, 162, 171, 175, 177
forecasting, 139
Funds Flow Statement, 108
Gross profit ratio, 103
Imprest system, 129
invoices, 32, 34, 38, 146, 180
Issued Share Capital, 96
Journal Entries, 41
liabilities, 38, 55, 56, 59, 82, 103, 104, 162, 172, 193
LIFO, 107
limited company, 94, 104
long term liabilities, 56
Ltd, 4, 25, 26, 27, 35, 75, 94, 98, 105, 178
manufacturing account, 74
margin, 119
mark up, 119
Memorandum of Association, 94
Net Profit ratio, 103
net worth, 56
nominal (general) ledger., 24
nominal value), 96
non-profit making organisations, 80
Omission, 42, 155
Opening stock, 45
ordinary shares, 96, 97, 98, 100
Original entry, 42, 155
Partnership, 84, 85, 88, 172
petty cash, 129
petty cash book, 129
petty cash vouchers, 129

Plc, 4, 94, 95, 98, 176
preference share, 96, 100
prepaid expenses, 52
Prime Cost, 75, 76, 80, 89, 94, 95, 96
prime costs, 74
Principle, 42, 155
private ledger, 24
Production Cost of completed goods, 76
production costs., 74
profit, 45
provision for bad (doubtful) debts, 70
Provision for Depreciation Account, 66
Prudence, 60, 69, 190
purchase (bought or creditors) ledger,, 24
purchase (bought/creditors), 34
purchases account, 19, 23, 26, 38, 149
purchases returns, 36
Rate of stock turnover, 104
receipts and payments account, 80
receivers, 94
REDUCING (DIMINISHING) BALANCE, 61
Refer to drawer, 123
reserve fund, 97
Return on capital employed, 103
returns inwards. *See* sales returns
Returns inwards. *See* sales returns

returns outwards. See purchase returns, See purchase returns
Returns outwards. *See* purchase returns
Revenue expenditure, 58
Reversal of entries, 42, 155
royalties, 74
Sales Account, 21, 29
sales day book, 32, 35
sales ledger, 24, 32, 34, 69
Sales Ledger Control Account, 34
Sales returns, 36, 47, 153
shares, 94, 95, 96, 97, 98, 99, 100, 104, 176, 177
Statement of Affairs, 114
straight line method, 60, 61, 65
surplus, 80
suspense account, 40, 41
THE REVALUATION METHOD, 61
trading certificate, 95
transposition of figures, 40
trial balance, 39, 40, 41, 42, 43, 50, 155
Turnover, 121
Unpresented cheques, 123
VAT Account, 33, 34
work in progress., 77
working capital, 56
Working capital, 55, 103, 162, 172, 193
write off a debt, 69

195

www.ingramcontent.com/pod-product-compliance
Lightning Source LLC
Chambersburg PA
CBHW020652220526
45464CB00001B/399